www.wadsworth.com

www.wadsworth.com is the World Wide Web site for Wadsworth and is your direct source to dozens of online resources.

At *www.wadsworth.com* you can find out about supplements, demonstration software, and student resources. You can also send email to many of our authors and preview new publications and exciting new technologies.

www.wadsworth.com
Changing the way the world learns®

Breaking and Entering

Burglars on Burglary

PAUL CROMWELL
Wichita State University

JAMES N. OLSON
University of Texas–Permian Basin

THOMSON
———
WADSWORTH

Australia • Canada • Mexico • Singapore • Spain
United Kingdom • United States

THOMSON
★
WADSWORTH
™

Senior Executive Editor, Criminal Justice:
Sabra Horne
Technology Project Manager: *Susan DeVanna*
Marketing Manager: *Dory Schaefer*
Advertising Project Manager: *Stacey Purviance*
Project Manager, Editorial Production:
Jennie Redwitz
Print/Media Buyer: *Karen Hunt*

Permissions Editor: *Sarah Harkrader*
Production Service: *Peggy Francomb,*
Shepherd, Inc.
Copy Editor: *Jean Pascual*
Cover Designer: *Yvo Riezebos*
Cover Image: *Will Crocker/Getty Images*
Compositor: *Shepherd, Inc.*
Text and Cover Printer: *Webcom*

For more information about our products,
contact us at:
Thomson Learning Academic Resource Center
1-800-423-0563

For permission to use material from this text,
contact us by:
Phone: 1-800-730-2214
Fax: 1-800-730-2215
Web: http://www.thomsonrights.com

Library of Congress Control Number:
2003100506

ISBN 0-534-62385-9

Wadsworth/Thomson Learning
10 Davis Drive
Belmont, CA 94002-3098
USA

Asia
Thomson Learning
5 Shenton Way #01-01
UIC Building
Singapore 068808

Australia/New Zealand
Thomson Learning
102 Dodds Street
Southbank, Victoria 3006
Australia

Canada
Nelson
1120 Birchmount Road
Toronto, Ontario M1K 5G4
Canada

Europe/Middle East/Africa
Thomson Learning
High Holborn House
50/51 Bedford Row
London WC1R 4LR
United Kingdom

Latin America
Thomson Learning
Seneca, 53
Colonia Polanco
11560 Mexico D.F.
Mexico

Spain/Portugal
Paraninfo
Calle/Magallanes, 25
28015 Madrid, Spain

To our wives and best friends,
Jimmie Cromwell and Cindy Ortloff Olson.

Contents

❖ Foreword

Did you ever want to talk to an "active" criminal about his (or her) motives for the crimes? Do you think you could obtain the kind of trust that would encourage an active criminal to talk to you candidly about committing crimes? Do you think you would have the courage to spend time with people who are active in street-level crime, hanging out with them where they live and work? Could you ask the kinds of questions that would elicit good and useful answers, and would you know the difference between answers that were the truth and those that were a part of "being conned"?

If we ever really want to understand crime, of course, it makes sense to talk to active criminals about their activity. That is not to say that criminals are necessarily experts about crime, but active criminals can tell us something valuable—something only they know—about their criminal ways. If we talk to them, we stand to learn something of great value. But we need to engage them effectively and study them correctly, or we stand to lose more than we gain.

It is also important to talk to "desisters"—people who used to be active in crime but have stopped. Talking to desisters can certainly tell us a great deal about the motives for crime, but it can also tell us, perhaps even more importantly, something about the motives for stopping. If one of our objectives in studying burglars is to find ways to ease burglars out of their criminal careers, then including desisters in the overall study will be a very important part of our work.

As editor of the *Wadsworth Contemporary Issues in Crime and Justice Series*, it is my great pleasure to announce *Breaking and Entering: Burglars on Burglary*, by Paul Cromwell and James N. Olson. The series is dedicated to the exploration

of important issues in crime and justice that receive limited attention in textbooks, but deserve closer study. Books appearing in this series are used by students to deepen their understanding of important questions facing the fields of criminology and criminal justice, and we are proud to say that the series has, over the years, published some of the most important books on current topics of interest to the field. This book is one of them.

Professors Cromwell and Olson have dedicated a significant portion of their careers to spending time with burglars—some who were still active as street criminals and some who had desisted from their criminal activity. They have talked to them during "time off," traveled with them at night when they typically "worked," and provided simulated scenarios about their approaches and decisions so that the intricacies of burglary could be better determined. Throughout this work, these two social scientists have been entirely scrupulous about the ethics of their research. They have been meticulous to be sure that they crossed no boundaries separating their observation from the criminal events they were interested in understanding.

This book is important because it is both groundbreaking about burglary and instructive about the limits of criminal justice policy. It is also an astonishing bit of social science, giving us an insider's view of crime that is rarely made possible.

When it first appeared, this book was a one-of-a-kind study of burglars because the authors talked to active burglars and asked them about their lives and their activity. Since its publication, there have been a couple of new studies that used a similar method to help us better understand this kind of crime, and this book incorporates the insights from new studies of burglars and drug use. But *Breaking and Entering* remains the best study of its type.

There are many points to ponder in this volume. What makes burglars decide to engage in crime, and how do they rationalize their acts? When going from house to house, how do they decide which one to burglarize? Why are drug abuse and burglary so closely intertwined, and how might our policies about the one kind of crime affect the propensity and severity of the other? Is burglary a good living for burglars? For fences? Are burglars that much different from you and me?

The most important contribution of this text is the way it helps us to see new avenues for burglary prevention. One of the big stories of the last twenty years in the United States is the systematic drop in burglary. Some of this drop has to do with "target hardening," as home security has improved and its prevalence greatly increased. But there is a panoply of other options, from dealing with fences to dealing with drug abuse, and the authors show us that there are many ways we can choose to reduce the incidence of burglary.

As books go, this is a small one. But after you read it you will realize that the weight of this book's contribution is far greater than its size. This book on burglars will inform your thinking about crime prevention in profound ways.

Todd R. Clear
Series Editor

Preface

❖

With this book we hope to make a valuable contribution to criminal justice literature: the secrets about how and why burglars go about doing their crimes and the lives they lead outside the law as learned from actual, working burglars. How do they go about the business of burglary? What factors do they take into account in selecting targets? How do they assess risk and gain? What might deter them from a specific criminal event? Once a burglary is committed, what do they do with their stolen goods? What factors might cause them to desist from crime or choose less risky criminal activity? This book can be used by academics, researchers, and professors, as well as in classrooms across the country where criminal behavior and crime causation are taught, namely criminology or criminal behavior courses or special topics courses in crime typologies.

What makes this book significant? It is based primarily on 18 months of field research conducted with 30 burglars in a southwestern metropolitan area of 250,000 population. All of these subjects were active burglars, meaning that they were in the community, committing burglaries regularly, often daily. This approach allowed us to obtain "real-world" information about burglars and burglary through the eyes of the offenders themselves. Readers can get inside the minds of the burglars and learn about them through their own words.

A specific purpose of the research was to determine the extent to which residential burglars utilized rational processes to select burglary targets

and what environmental factors were used as discriminative cues in the target selection process. Previous research in this area had not addressed this important factor, which could have significant policy and crime prevention implications.

We also sought to determine the effects of drug use on the rational choice decision model. Recent research (Wright and Decker, 1994; Bureau of Justice Statistics, 1997) suggests that as many as two-thirds of all burglars are addicted to drugs or have used drugs in the recent past. If drug usage affects the rational, sequential decision model of target selection by residential burglars, and if 60–70% of all burglars are drug abusers, decision-making models that assume a rational cognitive state are limited in explanatory power, predictive ability, and generalizability.

We were also concerned with whether the decision-making processes are modified or changed depending on whether or not the burglar is alone or working with accomplices. The literature in social psychology suggests that decisions made by groups are either more risky or more cautious than initial decisions made by individual members of the same group (Shaw, 1981). There is also evidence that group affiliation increases the drive level of group members and that performance on tasks requiring creativity or the use of judgment skills is impaired by the presence of coactors (Allport, 1920; Shaw, 1981; Zajonc, 1965, 1980). This suggests that burglars working with co-offenders may have a higher rate of offending than burglars working alone, and that they might experience impairment in their performance.

A further purpose of the study was to evaluate marketing or "fencing" strategies for stolen property as a corollary to burglary. Although there are several excellent studies of the professional fence (Klockars, 1974; Steffensmeier, 1986), there is less research on other avenues for the marketing of stolen property (see Henry, 1978). Our study assesses the behavior of criminal receivers of stolen property and attempts to describe the less well-known avenues of fencing stolen goods used by burglars.

Finally, we wished to assess to what extent the criminal justice system deters the residential burglar from initiating or continuing in a criminal career. We believe that our work will not only benefit academics and students in understanding the behaviors of criminals, but will also add to the body of research that positively influences crime prevention methods and means.

In addition to our own research, we have incorporated burglary research that was published after an earlier version of this book was completed. The research with residential burglars by Richard T. Wright and Scott H. Decker (1994) in St. Louis and Neal Shover (1996) in Tennessee has provided new insights, and in many cases, confirmed our findings. The addition of these studies provides a broader perspective to the overall study of burglars and burglary. We have expanded each chapter of the book to recognize new research and to incorporate our own evolving understanding of the burglary process and burglars' decision-making strategies.

ACKNOWLEDGMENTS

We take this opportunity to express our sincere appreciation for the support of the many persons who aided us in this endeavor. The inspiration for this study was the pioneering works of Professors C. Ray Jeffery, Paul and Patricia Brantingham, Neal Shover, Marcus Felson, Carl Klockers, Derek Cornish, and Ronald Clarke. We have also benefitted immeasurably from the scholarship and friendship of Scott Decker and Richard T. Wright, whose work on burglary and offender decision making is seminal.

In an earlier version of this book we had the benefit of working with D'Aunn Wester Avary, who began as a graduate assistant and became our co-author and valued colleague. She was a talented writer and skilled ethnographer. Her untimely death in 1995 has left a void in our lives that will not soon be filled. She was a true friend and inspirational colleague.

We would like to thank those who reviewed this book:

Shawna Cleary, University of Central Oklahoma
Mark Colvin, George Mason University
Mary Ann Eastep, University of Central Florida
Pat Faiella, University of Massachusetts, Boston
Edward L. Powers, University of Central Arkansas
David Struckhoff, Loyola University of Chicago
Boishu Wu, Sacramento State University

Finally, we must acknowledge our debt to the subjects of this study. These persons gave us their trust and provided us with insights we could never have obtained otherwise. Although they remain forever anonymous, we are grateful for their assistance.

Paul Cromwell
James N. Olson

1

❖

Introduction

This is a book about burglars and burglary. It is concerned with how offenders go about their business—the kinds of things they do or fail to do before and during the commission of a crime. It attempts to understand their perceptions of the risks and rewards involved in criminal activity, particularly in residential property crime. Of particular interest are their perceptions of the sanction threat of the criminal justice system and how those perceptions are formed and evolve, and are modified over time. It is further concerned with how residential burglars select targets; how the presence of co-offenders influences decision-making processes; and, how narcotics and drug abuse influence the prevalence and incidence of residential property crime, as well as what role drugs play in target selection and the risk–gain calculus employed by burglars.

The book is based primarily on 18 months of field research conducted in a southwestern metropolitan area of 250,000 population with 30 active burglars. One specific purpose of the research was to determine the extent to which residential burglars utilized rational processes to select burglary targets and what environmental factors were used as discriminative cues in the target selection process.

The second purpose of the study was to determine the effects of drug use on the rational choice decision model. Recent research (Wright and Decker, 1994; Bureau of Justice Statistics, 1997) suggests that as many as two thirds of all burglars are addicted to drugs or have used drugs in the recent past. Drug usage (and concomitant arousal and disequilibrium) affects the rational,

sequential decision model of target selection by residential burglars. Since 60 percent to 70 percent of all burglars are drug abusers, decision-making models that assume a rational cognitive state are limited in explanatory power, predictive ability, and generalizability.

The third purpose of the research was to determine how or by what processes decision making is modified or changed depending on whether or not the burglar is alone or working with accomplices. The literature in social psychology suggests that decisions made by groups are either more risky or more cautious than initial decisions made by individual members of the same group (Shaw, 1981). There is also evidence that group affiliation increases the drive level of group members and that performance on tasks requiring creativity or the use of judgment skills is impaired by the presence of coactors (Allport, 1920; Shaw, 1981; Zajonc, 1965, 1980). This suggests that burglars working with co-offenders may have a higher rate of offending than burglars working alone, and that they might experience impairment in their performance.

The fourth purpose of the study was to evaluate marketing or "fencing" strategies for stolen property as a corollary to burglary. Although there are several excellent studies of the professional fence (Klockars, 1974; Steffensmeier, 1986), there is less research on other avenues for the marketing of stolen property (see Henry, 1978). The present study assesses behavior of criminal receivers of stolen property and attempts to describe the less well-known avenues of fencing stolen goods by burglars.

The final purpose of the study was to assess to what extent the criminal justice system deters the residential burglar from initiating or continuing in a criminal career.

In this second edition, we have incorporated burglary research which was published after the first edition went to press. The research with residential burglars by Richard T. Wright and Scott H. Decker (1994) in St. Louis and Neal Shover (1996) in Tennessee has provided both new insights, and in many cases, confirmed our findings. The addition of these studies provides a broader perspective to the overall study of burglars and burglary.

THE METHODOLOGY: ISSUES RELATING TO ETHNOGRAPHIC RESEARCH

There is a large body of research that attempts to explore the factors taken into account by burglars in making the decision to offend and in selecting their targets. Many of these studies have been conducted in the ethnographic tradition: observing and talking to burglars about their attitudes, assumptions, perceptions, and beliefs, as well as the decision-making strategies and other aspects of their crimes. With limited exceptions, these studies have interviewed incarcerated burglars (Wright and Decker, 1994; Rengert and Wasilchick, 1985; Bennett and Wright, 1984; West, 1978). Although some researchers conclude that there is much to be learned from interviewing incarcerated offenders, others

are more cautious in attributing validity and reliability to data gathered from prisoners. One point of view is that criminals are not "natural" in a prison or police station, and the information obtained may be suspect. Some researchers argue that samples of incarcerated offenders are biased in favor of "failures" at crime. Others doubt the veracity (or the memory) of the informants. Wright and Decker add that many prisoners may not be truthful out of fear that providing such information might harm their chances for parole.

> Assurances of confidentiality notwithstanding, many prisoners remain
> convinced that what they say will affect their chances of being released
> and, therefore, they portray themselves in the best possible light. (p. 5)

Our burglar subjects were not incarcerated and the majority of them were not on probation or parole at the time of the study. They were active offenders, committing burglaries regularly. Using active offenders as research informants has both positive and negative implications. The ethnographic design allows the researcher to observe directly the behavior under study and to determine how offenders themselves view their criminal activities. The researcher frequently becomes part of the criminals' culture and environment and gets to know them in their natural setting (Glassner and Carpenter, 1985). The rich detail and insights obtained from such research provide not only knowledge of the world and activities of the offender, but also insight into "how it is possible that such a world and acts exist, and therefore, how it might be otherwise" (Glassner and Carpenter, p. 2).

On the other hand, locating active criminals in the free world who are willing to be interviewed or observed in action is difficult and time-consuming. If one can overcome this formidable barrier, however, the issues of validity and reliability of the data may be less problematic. As Glassner and Carpenter contend, it is easier for potential subjects to refuse access than to lie about their activities. Furthermore, information gathered from informants may be cross-checked with other informants, with official records, and even through judicious contact with victims. In many cases, police officials may be able to support or refute certain information provided by informants. For example, an informant discusses a burglary he or she committed, telling the interviewer about the planning, target selection process, when and where the burglary occurred, how entry was gained, and what was taken. Some of those facts can be checked—when, where, and how the burglar entered and what was taken. If that part of the information is found to be accurate, then the other information (planning process and decision strategies) can be viewed as more credible.

The ability to check these facts, and yet protect the identity of the informants, depends largely upon the relationship established between law enforcement officials and the researchers. This requires preresearch negotiations and agreements between law enforcement agencies and the research team. In most instances, without such agreements and assistance, the research will either be difficult to carry out or will require much more time to complete and may result in less credible data. Some argue that cooperation between police and the research team may taint the study, and possibly subject the informants to

criminal prosecution should they inadvertently become known to police through the process of validating information. Although this conceivably could occur, prudent planning can virtually eliminate the possibility.

Access to the Study Population

Not only may law enforcement agencies assist in cross-validating information gained from informants, they may also assist in making the initial contacts with persons in the criminal population sought by the researchers. Gaining entry and access to the desired criminal population (burglars, for example) is the most time-consuming and most difficult aspect of the study. McCall (1978) suggested that if researchers wanted to gain access to a criminal population, they should seek out persons (police officers, criminal lawyers, crime reporters, etc.) who might have contacts with the criminal population to be studied.

In obtaining a snowball sample[1] it is important to gain experienced and knowledgeable informants. A random sample is usually not possible or necessarily desirable. Carpenter and Glassner suggest that a purposive sample may be preferable. Previous research has generally agreed that a relatively small proportion of the criminal population commits a large proportion of all criminal acts (Chaiken and Chaiken, 1982; Johnson et al., 1985; Wolfgang, Figlio, and Sellin, 1972). The data suggest that this small group offends at a rate ten to fifteen times greater than that of other criminals. Thus, one high-incidence informant who has committed many crimes represents the experience (and knowledge) of several informants with lower individual crime rates. Therefore, it is important that the sample contains a significant number of these individuals. Although the sample should be generally representative of the criminal population, the inclusion of lower-rate offenders, novices, and juveniles (in some types of research) is appropriate.

One of the sampling problems we faced during the study involved prospective informants who were not really burglars by our operational definition, yet who initially deceived us about their qualifications. Because of the snowball technique, we added new informants regularly. As the word about the research spread through the drug-addict/criminal population of the community, some individuals perceived an opportunity to make a few dollars and enjoy a small scam at the same time. Although we were usually able to accept or disqualify a prospective informant after a short interview and/or after checking him or her out with other informants or through law enforcement contacts, a few managed to deceive us for a longer period. During a period late in the study we unknowingly snowballed into a group of "bottom of the barrel" junkies—addicts who subsisted through petty theft, scams, and minor drug dealing. These individuals were long-term, heavy users. They were not, however, burglars. Several knew enough about burglary from previous experience, and from street and jail talk, to convince us initially to accept them as informants. Sev-

[1]Snowball Sampling begins by selecting one or more initial research subjects who identify other persons who might be included in the study, who in turn identify others, and so on.

eral such subjects were referred to us by an informant already in the study. She received a $50 referral fee for each and, as we discovered later, she coached them in their effort to deceive us about their qualifications and took one half of the stipend that we paid them as informants. After the second interview (Session 2) we began to suspect that these three informants were not legitimate burglars. During Session 3 we confronted them and they admitted that they were not burglars and were participating for the stipend. During the course of the study several other informants were found to have lied about their qualifications. Only one of the fakers was discovered before the second interview. We were merely another of the many hustles these drug addicts depended upon to survive. There is a lesson here for ethnographers studying criminal behavior. It is relatively easy for a generic criminal to pretend to be a skilled burglar, armed robber, or drug dealer. Prison and jailhouse bull sessions and a lifetime of street talk have given them the ability to "talk a good crime." Only when the researcher actually goes into the field—into the social and physical environment of the subjects being studied—must the informant actually demonstrate any skills. From our experience, we believe that interview data gathered in jails, prisons, or from probation and parole populations may have serious validity problems.

In the present study, valuable information was obtained from three recent desisters. These were individuals who had been career criminals, but because of aging, the increasingly lengthy sentences imposed on them as their career progressed, or other reasons, had either given up crime as a lifestyle or had established new, less serious criminal activities (e.g., old-time burglars who were now shoplifting). These desisters were relatively easy to convince to become research informants because they were no longer "in the life" and in many cases had little to hide. They added a dimension to the research that was not often achieved by interviewing the active burglars. They could reflect, identify mileposts and turning points in their careers, and provide an overall criminal career perspective not available from those burglars at the beginning or in mid-career. We found that by reading transcripts of interviews with other burglars, they could provide valuable insights, as well as a type of validity check on the data gained from the other burglars. One such informant, crime-free for five years but considered by local law enforcement officers as "the most professional burglar ever to work this town," virtually became a consultant to the research team. Although he was never given access to the identities of the informants and he did not conduct interviews, much of the information obtained during the time he worked with us was filtered through him for comment. He would occasionally suggest new questions to ask or different avenues to explore with a particular informant. He would also periodically suggest that an informant was lying about something and recommend that we confront the informant about the inconsistency. Because he was almost invariably correct in his speculations, we avoided gathering a lot of inaccurate data.

Although they were technically not active burglars, the inclusion of desisters in the sample also gave us some insight into the process of functional displacement—career changes by offenders. Most of them had experienced

one or more career changes. Most had tried a legitimate job on several occasions; many had committed their crimes during both drug-free and heavy drug-using periods, and most had tried their hand at something other than burglary on occasion. Their perceptions of the impact of age and imprisonment on the criminal career added an unexpected dimension to the research, a perspective on how burglars (and presumably other criminals) may eventually desist from crime. Their insight into the motivations, perceptions, and actions of the younger, mid-career, active burglars gave us a richer understanding of the phenomenon of burglary.

PROBLEMS OF LAW AND ETHICS

One of the problems encountered in most criminological ethnographic research, particularly that conducted in the criminals' natural setting, is in obtaining valid data and observations without actually breaking the law or transgressing the somewhat more vague boundaries of professional ethics. These ethical and legal issues were particularly important and relevant in this study. We planned to reconstruct (or simulate) burglaries that the informants had committed which may or may not have been cleared. We wished to protect ourselves and our informants from possible criminal actions and ethical disquietude. We did not participate in planning or in discussing crimes to be committed in the future by our informants. We advised them orally and in writing that the promise of confidentiality would not extend to new crimes. We asked them to discuss only crimes that had been committed in the past. We justified our procedure on the basis that the crimes we studied had already been committed, and that we had no involvement in them whatsoever, except the knowledge gained later as to the identity of the perpetrator(s). No one (including the victim) was damaged further for our having knowledge of the identity of the guilty party. On the other hand, if the knowledge we gained allowed us to suggest more effective crime prevention strategies, society benefited.

We were concerned with the effects of drug use (altered states of arousal and equilibrium) on the decision-making processes of the informants. We therefore conducted interviews and ride-alongs (crime simulations or re-creations) with informants at various levels of drug arousal and at all hours. It was not unusual for one of us to be riding around town at 2:00 A.M. with two burglars who were high on drugs, or at 7:00 A.M. with a very sick heroin addict (note, we always drove the vehicle). We also faced the dilemma of having heroin addicts announce that they had to have a fix before they could go on with the interview and ask us to take them to their drug connection or to advance them money for heroin. We had previously stipulated that we would not loan money, make bail, or assist any informant if arrested. This proviso was a part of the oral agreement with the informants and was in writing as a part of the Voluntary Consent to Participate in Research that all informants read (or had read to

them) and signed. When informants requested a loan we reminded them of this agreement and repeated that we were "poor college professors" who did not carry much money with us. We also told them (regularly) that the money we paid them for interviews belonged to the university and that we did not have authority to loan or advance money. We did not want them to begin to think of us as potential robbery or burglary victims. This, for the most part, worked well. We did occasionally receive calls at home, at unusual hours, asking if we might be willing to interview them immediately because they needed money "to get their car fixed," or, in one case, "to get out of town in a hurry."

As trust and rapport developed between us and the informants some began to ask us to take them to their drug connections and wait while they got a fix. This began with a very articulate and professional burglar who was providing a wealth of information. He reported that he could not think straight until he got a fix and if we would just drive over to the "Tree" (a large oak tree in a local park known as a drug connection site), he would purchase his heroin, fix, and be ready to complete the interview in five minutes. Not willing to drive a burglar to his drug connection and yet wishing to know how an addict's decision varied immediately after a fix, we compromised. We drove the informant to a location two blocks from the address, dropped him off, and made an appointment to meet again in a half hour. That seemed satisfactory to the informant. We used the same technique during the remainder of the study when such circumstances arose.

Several burglars tested the limits of the relationship by asking permission to smoke marijuana while we drove around re-creating past crimes. We refused permission each time. We offered to drop them off for a while (to let them smoke) and come back to pick them up later. This approach did not seem to trouble the informants or diminish rapport.

Because the informants were active burglars and continuously arrestable, we expected that the attrition rate would be 25 percent to 30 percent. We discovered, however, that we had considerably underestimated attrition. Over 75 percent of the informants were arrested for some crime at least once during the course of the study. At first we feared that they might believe that their arrests were connected to their association with us. However, except for one almost disastrous incident, this did not seem to be the case. About midway into the study, at which point more than twenty subjects were involved in the interview process, local police obtained fifty-six sealed indictments as the result of an ongoing "sting" operation. We lost several informants to arrest in one night. After that night, there was a rumor going around for a while that we were part of the sting. We were fearful that someone might decide to retaliate against us, but we managed to convince most of them that we were as unaware of the sting as they (and we were) and eventually retained as informants almost all those arrested.

In general, we were able to resolve most of the problems that arose by using common sense and by being consistently honest with the informants. Because the research was the first of its type, there was little precedent for guidance.

METHOD

Selecting the Study Sample

As discussed earlier, the most critical step in ethnographic research with offenders is gaining access to the study population. It is not possible to place a notice in the newspaper asking for criminals to volunteer for the research. There is no sampling frame of criminals in the community from which to draw. And, even though the researcher might have knowledge of individuals who qualify for the study, he or she must develop trust and rapport with them before any study may begin. So, how is access to the study population gained and trust established?

Wright and Decker solved the problem of access by working with an ex-offender with extensive contacts among the street culture in St. Louis. They write:

The ex-offender hired to locate subjects for our project began by approaching former criminal associates. Some of these were still actively involved in various types of crimes, whereas others had retired or remained involved only peripherally through, for example, occasional buying and selling of stolen goods. . . He explained the research to the contacts, stressing that it was confidential and that the police were not involved. . . . (1994, p. 18)

We chose to initiate our sample population through a contact provided to us by a local burglary detective. He introduced us to a "confidential inform-ant," a female burglar with whom he had a relationship of trust. She became the source of the first few burglar informants, introducing us to her former husband and crime partner and to two other criminal associates. A probation officer, who was in our classes at the university, volunteered to assist us in locat-ing subjects and vouched for us to two of her former probationers, both of whom had recently discharged their probation terms. These five persons became the base of the snowball referral process.

They were promised complete confidentiality, anonymity, and a stipend of $50 for each active burglar referred by them and accepted for the study. The additional informants thus recruited were also promised confidentiality, anonymity, and a stipend of $50 for every interview, as well as an additional stipend for each additional, new active burglar they recruited. Informants who usually worked with partners (co-offenders) were encouraged to recruit their co-offenders. The initial three informants, who had worked with the researchers for a year during a pilot study, vouched for the researchers and ver-ified the nature of the research to those persons they recruited, who in turn did the same for those they referred.

Potential informants were screened to determine their qualifications. A potential informant was eligible to participate in the study if he or she admit-ted committing a minimum of two burglaries per month *and* satisfied two or more of the following requirements: (a) had been convicted by the courts or labeled by the police as a burglar, (b) perceived and labeled himself or herself

Table 1.1 Characteristics of Burglars: Frequency According to Ethnicity, Gender, and Drug of Choice

Drug of choice	White		Hispanic		African American		Total
	Male	Female	Male	Female	Male	Female	
Heroin	4	2	3	1	2	—	12
Cocaine	2	—	4	—	5	—	11
Alcohol	—	—	1	—	—	—	1
Marijuana	1	—	—	—	3	—	4
Methamphetamine (speed)	1	—	—	—	1	—	2
Total	8	2	8	1	11	0	30

as a burglar, and (c) was perceived or labeled by peers as a burglar. Four informants who had recently desisted—quit active burglary—were included in the sample. The final sample was composed of twenty-seven males and three females and was nearly evenly distributed among white, Hispanic, and African-American burglars. The mean age was twenty-five years; the range was sixteen to forty-three years. All of the burglars were drug addicts or abusers of illegal drugs. Table 1.1 presents the sample by drug of choice, gender, and ethnicity.

In labeling informants as "burglars," we recognize that they may (and probably do) commit a variety of other crimes. Research has shown that few offenders specialize in one criminal activity. However, our informants considered burglary their primary criminal activity. The following comment was typical of most of the subjects we interviewed: "I'm mostly a burglar, you know. That's what I'm good at. Sometimes I do other stuff, like boosting or dealing a little, but burglar is what I am. You can ask anybody in the Flats [a low-income high crime area of the community]. They'll tell you that I'm a burglar." Wright and Decker came to similar conclusions. Many of the informants in their St. Louis research considered burglary their "main line" and they seldom considered alternative offenses when faced with a need for money. As one of their subjects stated: "I guess the reason why I stick with burglary is because it makes me a lot of money . . . I guess you could say why I just do burglary is because I've been doing it a while and I'm kind of stuck with it" (pp. 51–52).

Our informants occasionally resorted to other crimes when a situation presented itself. Although some shoplifted and others bought and sold stolen property or sold drugs, they relied primarily on burglary, as one subject related, for their "usual gig."

Staged Activity Analysis

There are two generally accepted methods for the collection of data in an ethnographic design: (a) observation, and (b) the ethnographic interview (Glassner and Carpenter). Entering the burglars' world as a participant and observing their behavior from that vantage point would provide insights that

could not be gained through other research strategies. Legal and ethical problems, however, generally preclude such an approach. On the other hand, ethnographic interviews with criminal subjects about their own criminal behavior frequently produce misleading results.

We selected an alternative strategy: one that we termed *staged activity analysis*. The subjects were asked to reconstruct and simulate their past burglaries as nearly as possible in the same manner in which they were originally committed. We observed, questioned, and recorded the events and answers. Although the burglars reconstructed the crimes they had previously committed, they did not actually commit the crime again. Most legal and ethical problems involved in conducting the research were eliminated through this technique. Staged activity analysis consists of extensive interviews and "ride-alongs," during which the informants were asked to discuss and evaluate residential sites they had previously burglarized, and sites previously burglarized by other informants in the study. Each informant participated in as many as nine sessions with the researchers.

The initial session with each burglar consisted of a semi-structured interview three to four hours in duration. During this session each subject was asked a series of open-ended questions ranging from queries about how he or she began as a burglar, to specific questions about cues, motivations, probing strategies (casing), and disposing (fencing) of stolen goods. The remaining eight sessions involved actual visits to sites previously burglarized by the informant and other informants in the study. Sessions were conducted under all conditions in which burglars might conceivably commit their crimes: in the daytime, at night, with an informant alone, with informants grouped with their usual co-offenders, when using drugs, when stable, and when needing a drug administration (withdrawing). Before each session the informants were asked to estimate their own drug state at the time of the session and to recall their drug state at the time of the actual burglary of the site. An informant's drug state was estimated as follows:

1. Nonuser

2. Aroused: in need of a drug administration (sick or in the early stages of withdrawal)

3. Regular user/stable: having administered a drug recently and in no immediate need of another drug administration

4. Regular user/high: having administered a drug recently and feeling intoxicated, stoned, high, or nodding off

5. Intermittent user/stable: no drugs in the past twelve hours and no immediate need for drugs

6. Intermittent user/high: not a regular user but having administered a drug recently and feeling intoxicated, stoned, high, or nodding off

During sessions which involved ride-alongs (simulations and reconstructions of burglaries) the subjects were asked to direct the interviewer to the site of a recent burglary, using the method of travel and route taken at the time of

the actual burglary. The informants were asked to recall why they had chosen that specific route and neighborhood or area of the city.

Upon arriving in the general neighborhood of the target site the subjects were instructed to proceed to the target site in as nearly as possible the same manner as they had at the time of the actual burglary. At the target site, the informants were asked a series of open-ended questions relating to the burglary, with emphasis on salient and subtle cues relied upon to select the target, including cues relating to occupancy, potential gain, and perceived risks. The informants were also queried about probes used to determine occupancy, method of entry, techniques of searching, division of labor (if co-offenders were involved), what was taken, the route and method of escape, how the stolen property was converted to cash or drugs, and how any money obtained by disposing of the stolen property was spent. Open-ended questions were pursued in detail depending upon the informants' willingness and ability to discuss each specific topic.[2]

We found that many of the subjects were unable to articulate the cues they relied on in making a target selection decision. Like Justice Potter Stewart's comment on pornography, they seemed to know a good site when they saw one, but could not explain why. As one burglar subject explained: "I can't tell you why man, I just have a feeling about this place. It don't look good. I wouldn't do it."

Another informant exclaimed: "This is a good one. I'd do it in a New York minute. . . . It's just a gut feeling."

In order to assist them in articulating their decision process, we asked the burglar subjects to drive or walk through the immediate neighborhood and select a residence that they considered a *high-risk* site, that is, one that they were very unlikely to burglarize, and another that they considered *low-risk*—vulnerable to burglary. After selecting the two sites, they were asked if they could tell us how the two sites differed. Most could do so. Comparing the two sites seemed to facilitate their ability to articulate the factors that went into the decision.

In subsequent sessions, the informants were driven to at least two sites previously burglarized by other informants and to at least two sites selected by other informants as high risk. For each previously burglarized site and its matched high-risk site, the informant was asked to rate the site in terms of its vulnerability and attractiveness as an immediate burglary target given the circumstances that prevailed at the time of the staged activity analysis. The sites were rated on a scale of 0 to 10. An *attractiveness rating* of zero meant, "Under the circumstances that are present now, I would *not* burglarize this residence." A rating of 10 meant, "This is a very attractive and vulnerable target and I would definitely take steps to burglarize it *right now*." In addition, each informant was presented with two hypothetical situations and asked to provide an attractiveness rating for each: (1) If you knew no one was at home at this residence, what rating would you give the site on attractiveness as a burglary target *right now*; and (2) if you knew no one was home *and* you knew that there

---

[2]A more detailed account of the research methodology is found in Appendix B.

was $250 in cash inside, what rating would you give the residence on its attractiveness as a burglary target *right now?*

Prior research and knowledge gained from police sources indicates that a high percentage of burglars commit their offenses with one or more partners. This suggests that interviews and burglary reconstructions should include the burglar's co-offenders. Research has long concluded that behavior is affected by others—facilitating or inhibiting individual actions (Shaw, 1981; Zajonc, 1965, 1980; Allport, 1920). Therefore, subsequent sessions included the subject's crime partners, if available. The purpose of these sessions was to determine to what extent, if any, group decisions differed from individual decisions. During group sessions the informants were asked to provide individual attractiveness ratings of the various sites without discussion with their co-offender(s). The informants were then encouraged to discuss the target site with their co-offender(s) and arrive at a group attractiveness rating. The drug state of each member was determined prior to evaluating the sites.

At the conclusion of nine sessions the burglars and their co-offenders had evaluated up to twenty-one previously burglarized sites and their matched high-risk counterparts. Three hundred and ten session hours with thirty active burglars were conducted. Each session was tape-recorded and verbatim transcripts were made.

A quantitative substudy was conducted to validate the ethnographic data obtained from the burglar informants. The study consisted of comparing 300 burglarized residences to 300 nonburglarized residences. The burglarized residences were obtained by selecting every n^{th} case from the records of burglaries reported to the local police during the two preceding years. The nonburglarized residences were selected by taking every n^{th} residential building from the city tax rolls. The tax roll residences were screened by comparing them to burglary reports from the appropriate year. Residences that reported burglaries during the two-year period under consideration were eliminated until 300 residences with no reported burglaries for the two-year period were obtained.

Each burglarized and nonburglarized residence was evaluated in terms of its attributes on the following variables: distance from corner, distance from stop sign, distance from traffic light, distance from school, distance from commercial business establishment, distance from park, distance from church, distance to nearest four-lane street, number of lanes of traffic in front of residence, average speed of traffic in front of residence, and presence or absence of garage or carport. A discriminant analysis was performed to determine which variables best discriminated between burglarized and unburglarized residences.

In the chapters that follow we present the burglars' perspective regarding the decision to offend, target selection, deterrent value of the criminal justice process, factors that facilitate burglary and those that inhibit their actions. We also consider the role of the receiver of stolen property (the fence) in property crime, the process of desisting or quitting crime, and we discuss crime prevention strategies that focus on deterring the burglar.

2

❖

The Reasoning Offenders' Motives and Decision-Making Strategies

M uch of the recent research in environmental criminology, particularly crime-specific studies (Shover, 1991, 1996; Shover and Honaker, 1992; Wright and Decker, 1994; Jacobs, 1999; Tunnell, 1992; Shachmurove, Fishman, and Hakin, 1997) has focused on the rational processes by which an offender chooses a criminal career, selects targets, and carries out criminal acts. Rational choice theory is predicated on the assumption that individuals *choose* to commit crimes. The theory predicts that individuals evaluate alternative courses of action, weighing the possible rewards against the costs and risks, and choosing the action that maximizes their gain.

The notion of rational choice has its origins in both the classical theories of Cesare Beccaria and Jeremy Bentham in the late eighteenth century and in relatively recent economic theory, specifically in the work of Gary Becker (1968). According to classical theory, criminals are free, rational, and hedonistic. They choose among alternative courses of action according to their perceptions of the risks and gains associated, seeking to maximize gain (or pleasure) and minimize risk (or pain).

Modern classical explanations are derived from economic theory, which views the decision to commit crime as essentially like any other decision—that is, one made on the basis of a calculation of the costs and benefits of the action. The benefits of a criminal action are the net rewards of crime and include not only the gains but also intangible benefits such as emotional pleasure or satisfaction. The individual may receive immense satisfaction from the excitement of crime, from the independent lifestyle afforded by crime, or

from outwitting the authorities. The risks or costs of crime are those associated with formal punishment should the individual be discovered, apprehended, and convicted, as well as psychological or social costs, such as pangs of conscience, social disapproval, marital and family discord, or loss of self-esteem (Vold and Bernard, 1986).

The degree of rationality that can be attributed to offenders in planning and executing their crimes and how rationality is related to crime prevention measures have been central issues of debate (Clarke and Cornish, 1985, 2001; Cornish and Clarke, 1986; Cornish, 1993; Cook, 1980). Brezina (2002) characterizes the major positions as the "narrow" and the "wide" models of rational choice. The narrow model assumes that offenders consider all possible consequences of their actions and choose the course that maximizes their personal gain and utility. The wide model, in contrast, suggests that offenders do not operate under optimal conditions; that the complete range of possible consequences is always unknown to the actor, and that even if all possible consequences were known, most individuals are not capable of the intricate and complex calculations necessary to choose the course of action to maximize outcomes. In other words, the wide model assumes that information necessary to make good decisions is frequently unavailable and that even if it were available, most people are not particularly competent decision makers.

This concept of "limited rationality" proposes that for behavior to be rational, it does not have to be carefully preconceived and planned or require hierarchical, sequential decision making. It is enough that decisions are perceived to be optimal. It does not require deliberate weighing of carefully considered alternatives and consequences. It is sufficient that decision makers choose between alternatives based upon their immediate perception of the risks and gains involved. The decision does not have to be the best possible under the circumstances, nor does it have to be based upon an accurate assessment of the situation. A burglar can never calculate with assurance the value of the property he or she expects to take away in a burglary or know with confidence the extent of the punishment should he or she be apprehended. The concept of limited rationality recognizes the limited capacity and willingness of most persons to acquire and process information from more than one input or source simultaneously.

Cornish and Clarke (1986) concluded that people usually pay attention to only some of the facts or sources at their disposal, employing shortcuts or rules of thumb to speed the decision process. These rules of thumb are analogous to Cook's (1980) concept of "standing decisions," which negate the need to weigh carefully all the alternatives and consequences before making a decision in many cases. A standing decision may simply be a decision made beforehand to take advantage of certain types of criminal opportunities or to avoid others. In effect, these are rational processes that do not require conscious analysis each time they are employed.

In this chapter we consider the rational processes that motivate offenders to commit burglary and the decision strategy they use in committing the crime. When considering the motives that underlie crime, we must first differentiate

between *criminality* and *crime*. Crime refers to the criminal event itself. Criminality refers to processes through which individuals originally become involved in crime and which create a "readiness" to offend. Clarke and Cornish (1985) identify such factors as temperament, intelligence, broken homes, parental crime, self-perception, criminal associates, etc. as being involved in the development of readiness to commit crimes. Cornish and Clarke (1986, p. 2) assert that the development of criminality is a process that is usually multi-staged and extends over an extended period of time. For example, a person from a broken home might not develop adequate social bonds allowing him or her to perceive of theft as a reasonable means of dealing with an urgent need for cash. Having associates who commit criminal acts might further cement the perception that crime is an appropriate solution to the problem. For purposes of this study, we assume a readiness to commit crimes and we do not delve into the dynamics of the burglar's criminality. Of more immediate concern are those variables that translate the readiness into a criminal event—from predis-posing an individual to criminal activity to precipitating the actual event.

MOTIVATION FOR BURGLARY

The motivation that drives the burglary event is a consistent factor in the literature. Bennett and Wright (1984, p. 31) found that burglars' motivations fell into six major categories. In order of importance, they are:

1. Instrumental needs
2. Influence of others
3. Influence of presented opportunities
4. None (the individual is constantly motivated)
5. Expressive needs
6. Alcohol

Scarr (1973) found that burglars in his study cited four general motives; in order of importance:

1. Need for money to buy drugs
2. Need for money to lead a "fast expensive life"
3. Social motives (gangs, delinquent subcultures, peer approval, status)
4. Idiosyncratic motives (kicks, thrills, pathological behavior, rebellion)

Reppetto's (1974) subjects reported satisfaction of their need for money as the primary motivation for their robberies and burglaries. Subsidiary satisfactions such as excitement, revenge, and curiosity were cited by a significant but smaller percentage of the subjects. Excitement as a motive was mentioned most often by the younger burglars and less often by the older. Only 10 percent of Reppetto's subjects stated that they would continue to commit burglary if their need for money, including money for drugs, was satisfied (p. 22).

Rengert and Wasilchick (1985) concluded, "The primary reason stated by burglars we interviewed for deciding to commit a burglary was simply to obtain money. . . . The need for money arose out of psychologically defined needs, not subsistence needs" (p. 54).

Wright and Decker reported that the decision to commit a burglary was driven primarily by a need for cash. Due to the "then and there" lifestyle of most thieves—living entirely in the present—getting a job and working for the money was not a viable alternative. They explained that much of the offending by the burglars in their study was directed toward obtaining the funds necessary to sustain activities that constituted the essence of "streetlife" (pp. 194–5).

Shover (1996) argues that the lives of burglars and other thieves is one of an unending "party." Their crimes are committed to allow them to maintain a lifestyle that is essentially the pursuit of a pattern of activities that they experience as pleasurable (p. 93). They are seeking to "keep the party going." Shover states that those who live this lifestyle share a minimal concern for serious matters in favor of enjoying the moment (p. 94):

> Persistent thieves spend much of their criminal gains on alcohol and other drugs. The proceeds of their crimes "typically" are used for personal, non-essential consumption, rather than, for example, to be given to family or used for basic needs. . . . Thieves and hustlers spend many of their leisure hours enjoying good times, albeit there is a decidedly frenetic and always precarious quality to the way these times are lived (p. 94). In an early study of theft and thieves, Jackson (1969) wrote: [Burglars] if the had any money . . . [they] wouldn't be out stealing, they'd be partying. It's as simple as that. If they have money they're partying and when they're broke, they start stealing again.

Our subjects lived similar lives and expressed similar motives for their crimes. They stressed the need for money to fulfill expressive needs as the primary motivation for their offending. Only one burglar in our study reported a primary need for money for something other than to purchase drugs or alcohol or for other "partying" activities—and he used the money to support his gambling habit. Although virtually every burglar used some of the money from criminal activity to buy food and clothing and to pay for shelter, transportation and other licit needs, the greatest percentage of the proceeds from burglary went toward the purchase of drugs and alcohol and to the activity they loosely labeled as partying. Many of the burglars discussed the importance of maintaining a "fast, expensive life." Keeping up appearances was stressed by many as a primary concern. This was especially true for the African-American burglars. One burglar summed up the attitude this way: "You gotta understand about blacks. It's important to keep up a front, to have money and for people to know you have money. Looking good is important. You can't get women if you don't have some bread."

All thirty of our burglar subjects abused drugs and/or alcohol. Most were addicts. Some were so addicted that they took their stolen items directly to a

local drug dealer who was known to trade drugs for quality stolen goods. They did not want to spend the extra time converting their goods to cash before buying drugs. Most, however, converted their loot to cash and then went immediately to a drug dealer or to a bar where they ingested or self-administered their way into temporary oblivion. The length of their "party" determined the time span between burglaries, for when they ran out of drugs and alcohol and had "slept it off," they began again the search for a new burglary target.

We recognize that our sample was not an exact reflection of the nation's population of residential burglars insofar as drug and alcohol abusers may have been overrepresented. However, Shover (1971; 1996) and Wright and Decker arrived at similar conclusions concerning the lifestyles of burglars and other thieves. Reppetto also noted that a large percentage of the burglars he studied had histories of prior drug and alcohol abuse. He concluded that, "increase of drug use seems most strongly correlated with recent increases in residential burglary rates" (p. 23).

Jerry, one of our more articulate burglar subjects, summed it up as follows:

Once I got into the life, I liked it—a lot. I always liked to party and if you party you can't keep a job for any length of time. I like the ladies too. And the ladies like dudes with lots of folding money. You can't keep it up working for hourly wages. I've had some pretty good jobs before, but it was never enough. Not enough money. Not enough time. Not enough freedom—when you work. Now I work for myself. I'm a self-employed thief. I can party all I want to and when I run out of green, I go get some more.

While drugs, alcohol, and "party" were the dominant motives for the burglars in our study, other factors also played a role for some burglars. Excitement and thrills were mentioned by almost every informant; however, only a few would commit a burglary for that purpose only. Like Reppetto, we concluded that the younger, less experienced burglars were more prone to commit crimes for thrills and excitement. Gerald, a twenty-year-old burglar stated: "I used to love that adrenaline rush you get when you first go in the window. It's as good as coke. Heart starts thumping and you get shaky and feel super alive. When I was fifteen, sixteen years old, I lived for that feeling. I still get scared and get the rush, but now I do it [burglarize] for money."

Another informant, Steve, a thirty-six-year-old, said: "There's no feeling like it. It's fear and sex and danger and every other exciting feeling you ever had all rolled into one. I'd do crime just for that rush. I *do* do crime just for that rush. Sometimes."

About 30 percent of the informants reported committing at least one burglary for revenge. They seldom obtained much material reward in revenge burglaries, reporting instead that they "trashed" the victim's house. This tendency was more pronounced among burglars under twenty-five years of age. One burglar reported: "I was helping this friend move into a new house and the white lady next door saw that we were black. I heard her tell another neighbor that she was upset about a black man moving in next door. I decided to come back the next day and 'do' her house for revenge."

Another said that he had burglarized the house of a former friend after that individual had "snitched" on him. He said: "I didn't take nothin' except some food. Mainly I just trashed his place. I was really pissed off."

THE DECISION STRATEGY
AND TARGET SELECTION

Being motivated to commit a crime is a necessary but not a sufficient condition for the actual commission of the act. Even a highly motivated burglar—one who has immediate need for money—must still locate a vulnerable target and manage to effect entry without detection. These tasks are not as simple as they may appear to be. As Wright and Decker observe, "In theory, the supply of residential properties seems so vast that finding a target would seem to be a simple matter. In practice, however, potential targets are fairly limited" (p. 62). The potential burglary target must:

- Be unoccupied (90 percent of the burglars we interviewed stated that they would not knowingly enter a residence where they knew someone was at home)
- Not be easily observed from the street of neighboring homes
- Be in a neighborhood or area where the burglar would not "stand out" or be noticed as a suspicious stranger
- Be accessible—relatively easy to break-in to
- Contain items worth stealing

Gerald, an experienced burglar explained:

First off, you gotta find a place that's empty; you know, no one's home. Sometimes it's hard to tell. Place look empty but you go check it out and there's somebody there. One time I rang the doorbell to see if anybody was home at this one house and nobody answered, so I go in the back and break in through the sliding door. Next thing I know there's this old lady sleeping in front of the TV. I got the hell out of there. . . . Sometimes you can check out a whole bunch of places and none look good.

Jerry, an African-American burglar agreed: "It ain't easy . . . looking for places to hit. Me, I gotta pretty much stay in neighborhoods where I fit in. Some of these rich white neighborhoods are too dangerous. I stand out . . . people watch me and if I hang around too long, somebody be calling the law."

Interestingly, during the initial interview virtually every burglar in our study reported a rational decision-making strategy in selecting burglary targets. The following dialogue is typical of responses during the first interview:

Q. *Before you decide to break into a house, what kinds of things do you think about—I mean what makes you decide whether a house is a good place to burglarize or too risky?*

A. First, I gotta case the place. Sometimes I watch the place for two, three days before I go in.
Q. Really? You take that much time? What are you looking for?
A. Fuckin' A! Can't be too careful. I'm looking for, you know, when they come and go, and how many people live there, when the police come by, have they got good stuff You know; is it going to be worth it to hit the place?

But, when we went with them to reconstruct their past crimes, we found important variations between what they initially told us (in the relatively structured interview setting of Session 1) about the process of selecting a target and committing a burglary, and what they actually did when presented with a field simulation. Most of our burglars could design a textbook burglary. However, when subsequently visiting sites of burglaries they had previously committed, the characteristics of the target sites and the techniques used to burglarize those targets were seldom congruent with the completely rational approach they had constructed during the initial interview. The sites, more often than not, were targets of opportunity rather than purposeful selections. There were three common patterns:

1. The burglar happened by the potential burglary site at an opportune moment when the occupants were clearly absent and the target was perceived as vulnerable (open garage door, windows, etc.)

2. The site was one that had been previously visited by the burglar for a legitimate purpose (as a guest, delivery person, maintenance worker, or other such activity)

3. The site was chosen after "cruising" neighborhoods searching for a criminal opportunity and detecting some overt or subtle cue as to vulnerability or potential for material gain

One of the purposes of the study was to determine which environmental cue or complexes of cues caused a burglar to perceive of a potential burglary target as vulnerable to burglary. Some environmental criminologists (Bennett and Wright; Brantingham and Brantingham, 1978, 1981; Brown and Altman, 1981) have focused on the burglar's use of distinctive environmental stimuli that function as signals or cues to provide salient information about the environment's temporal, spatial, sociocultural, psychological, and legal characteristics. An individual who is motivated to commit a crime uses these discriminative cues to locate and identify target sites. With practice the individual gains experience and learns which discriminative cues and which combination or sequence of cues are associated with "good" targets. These cues then serve as a "template," which is used in victim or target selection. Potential victims or targets are compared to the template and either rejected or accepted, depending on the congruence (Brantingham and Brantingham, 1978, 1991, 1993). In effect, these are standing decisions that do not require conscious analysis each time they are employed. Regardless of whether the individual is consciously aware of the construction and implementation of the template, each time it is

successfully employed it is reinforced and becomes relatively automatic. The Branthinghams state:

> The templates are not a simple list of easily identifiable and measurable characteristics, but more a holistic image with a complex interaction of past and relationships seen from varying perspectives. (1993:12)

As one of our burglary subjects said: "I just know how I feel about it. I drive around and see a place and think, 'This is a good one.' It's experience—know what I'm saying? I been doing this a long time and I just know."

Another burglar informant perhaps stated it better. He said: "I got a criminal mind, you know. Something just tells me a place is hot or cold. It's like intuition."

Finding that most burglars have developed an intuitive mental template of what constitutes a good or a bad burglary target, we set out to determine which discriminative cues or sequence of cues composed the template. Knowing what cues cause a site to be more or less attractive to a burglar should allow development of effective burglary prevention strategies.

We also wished to understand the decision-making processes involved. How does the burglar use cues that represent risk and gain? What factors might cause a burglar to be deterred from burglary? What makes a site more attractive to the burglar? What are the cues that the burglar uses to makes the decision to commit the burglary? How does the burglar determine whether a target site is unoccupied? Is there a favored time of day, or day of the week? How does he or she effect entry into a locked residence?

Interviews with our thirty burglar subjects and the re-creations of past burglaries by the subjects suggest that a burglar's decision to "hit" a specific target is based primarily on environmental cues that are perceived to have immediate consequences. Most burglars seem to attend only to the present; future events or consequences do not appear to weigh heavily in their risk-versus-gain calculation. Drug-using burglars and juveniles are particularly oriented to this immediate-gain and immediate-risk decision process. Non-drug-using experienced burglars are probably less likely to attend only to immediate risks and gains. Our informants, although experienced burglars, were all drug users, and tended to have a "here and now" orientation toward the rewards and costs associated with burglary. As one informant stated:

> *I don't think about the future. Today is all that counts with me. You might be dead tomorrow, so live the best you can right now, today. I knew this dude that was always planning what he was gonna do someday—how he was gonna have a big car and a house and be rich and stuff—he got killed by some other dudes in a dope deal. All that planning didn't do no good for him. Wasted all that time, you know. I don't think that way.*

Another burglar assessed his life in the following manner: "Everyday I live past fifteen, sixteen years old is just luck. I don't expect to get to twenty-five or thirty. I just ain't goin' to worry about what might happen. I'm just goin' to have a good time while I'm here."

And another stated: "I don't think about it. I might think about it later, but when I'm doing a crime, I worry about the here and now. The police and the joint aren't part of my thinking, you know what I mean. Can't let those things bother you."

These findings suggest that the rational choice process must be considered as it is perceived through the eyes of the offender. Long-term rewards and future punishment appear to have little effect on most burglars. They are concerned about danger at the crime site and the immediate rewards to be had there.

ASSESSING GAIN

There is considerable research supporting the position that reward or gain is the most important element in the decision to commit a burglary. Shover (1996) found that instead of paying close attention to the potential consequences of their actions and planning carefully to avoid arrest, offenders tend to focus on the money that committing a crime will yield and how they will spend that money. Shover cited one subject, who stated:

"I didn't think about nothing but what I was going to do when I got that money and how I was going to spend it, you know. See, you're not thinking about those things [possibility of being arrested]. You're thinking about that big paycheck at the end of thirty or forty minutes of work." (1996, pp. 158–9)

The decision strategy employed by our informants began with an appraisal of the circumstances at the potential target site. Most burglars in the study expended minimal energy and time assessing gain cues. They estimated potential gain quickly and intuitively. They tended to make assessments of individual target sites based upon their evaluation of the general affluence of the neighborhood in which the target is located. The assumption is that most residences in a neighborhood contain essentially the same quality and quantity of "stealable" items. As one burglar stated: "It don't take no Einstein to know [what's in a house]. I can look at a neighborhood and almost tell you what's in every house there. Poor neighborhoods got poor stuff. Rich neighborhoods got rich stuff."

Luis, a heroin addict/burglar, told the interviewer: "Most houses in this neighborhood have got at least two color TVs, a VCR, some stereo equipment, and some good jewelry. A lot of 'em have got guns, too."

Wright and Decker found that almost all of the offenders in their study were attracted to residences "which, judging from the outside, appeared to them to contain 'good stuff.'" The most obvious cue was the size of the house. "Other things being equal, a large house was regarded as promising the biggest payoff" (Wright and Decker, p. 82). Well-maintained property was considered by their burglar informants to contain the most desirable goods. The type of car parked in the driveway was also a gain cue to the subjects in Wright and Decker's study. One of their subjects stated: "Here's this big old house sittin' up there and in the driveway is two BMWs and a Mercedes. This

other house might have a van or something like that . . . So I visualize that [the intended target] must have more things than that house." (pp. 82–3).

Our burglar subjects expressed similar preferences. Donna stated: "I'm always looking for signs that they got something worthwhile. Big expensive houses, rich cars, stuff like that."

Another subject expressed a preference for houses in a certain part of town where the lots were all over an acre in size and the houses large and expensive. He said:

These people mostly have gardeners and other people doing their work for them. When I see somebody moving that ain't the owners and a gardener's truck parked in the street and lots of expensive trees and flowers, I know these people got money. Top of that, if I go on the property people next door and passing by probably goin' to think I work there.

Inside Information

In some cases, the assessment of gain does not require use of the mental template. The burglar actually knows what is inside the house through the use of informants who have been in the house and have given inside information to the burglar. Experienced burglars often work with insiders who have access to potential targets and advise the burglar about things to steal. They may also provide such critical information as times when the owner is away and of weaknesses in security. One female informant maintained close contact with several women who worked as maids in affluent sections of the community. She would gain the necessary information from these women and later come back and break into the house, often entering by a door or window left open for her by the accomplice. A more common scenario was for the burglar to learn of the habits and activities of home owners from maids, gardeners, and others who had no intention of knowingly assisting a burglar. Friends who worked in these jobs would alert him to possible burglaries through casual talks about their job or their employer, mentioning, for instance, that the family they worked for was leaving for a two-week vacation, or that they had just purchased a new television or VCR. The burglar then used that otherwise innocent information to commit a burglary.

People involved in a variety of service jobs (repair, carpet cleaning, pizza delivery, lawn maintenance, plumbing, carpentry) enter many homes each day and have the opportunity to assess the amount and quality of potential stolen merchandise and security measures taken by the residents. Burglars will often establish contact with employees of these businesses for purposes of obtaining this inside information. One informant said: "My homie, he works for _____ [a carpet cleaning service] and he in five, six different houses every day. He always keeps an eye out for places where they have expensive stuff. I give him somethin' off every job if the clues me in to a place."

One of the burglars in our study worked closely with an employee of a maid service. The maid provided information to the burglar about security,

times when the residents were away from home, and a list with specific locations of valuable goods inside the house.

Information about potential targets was frequently gained from fences—persons who purchase stolen property for later resale. Because many fences have legitimate occupations, they may have knowledge of the existence of valuable property from social or business relationships. They can often provide the burglar with information about the owners' schedules and the security arrangements at the target site (see Chapter 5, "Burglars and Fences," for a more detailed discussion). Pawnshop employees may also be able to provide burglars with information about potential targets. One professional burglar told the interviewer that an employee at a pawnshop provided him with copies of jewelry appraisals and the addresses of potential targets.

Inside knowledge is also obtained by persons who work regularly in a neighborhood but who never actually enter a potential target residence. Several of our informants worked sporadically as carpenters' helpers or roofers. During the course of residential construction jobs they became aware of the habits of the people living nearby. They used this knowledge later or provided inside information to other burglars for a fee or a split of the take. Larry, a burglar and heroin addict, told us:

> One time I was working on this roofing job in this real nice area. I got to know the schedules of almost everybody on the block. I knew when they left in the morning and came home at night, and who stayed home during the day. About two weeks after the job was done I came back and did [burglarized] almost every house on that block.

ASSESSING RISK

The risk side of the decision-making equation is one of the most difficult to study and one of the most controversial. Do burglars carefully plan their crimes? Do they act spontaneously, taking advantage of opportunity? Do they act without giving thought to short-term or long-term risk? The answer to these questions is central to developing burglary prevention strategies. While it may be difficult for a homeowner to hide or disguise indicators of gain, such as affluence of neighborhood, size of residence or type of automobile driven, controlling risk cues may be more easily accomplished.

As stated earlier, consideration of long-term risk is almost nonexistent in the decision processes of most burglars (however, see Chapter 6, "Desisting from Burglary," for a significant exception to this rule). Burglars and many other criminals tend to live in the here and now. Not only do they not consider next month or next year, most do not even consider next day. On the other hand, immediate risks do play a significant role in target selection. Shover (1996) found that "burglars pay close attention to whether or not a residence is occupied and how easily potential entry points can be seen by neighbors and passers-by" (p. 161).

We learned that while most burglars stated a preference for the homes of the affluent as presenting the greatest opportunity for gain, they tended to avoid these houses and neighborhoods due to increased risk. Affluent homes are more likely to have alarm systems and private security patrols, as well as to be occupied during the day by residents and/or servants. Burglars also perceived themselves as more likely to "stand out"—to be noticed and observed—in such neighborhoods. One of the burglars interviewed for a study by George Rengert (1989), commenting on the possibility of committing a burglary in a very affluent neighborhood near Philadelphia, remarked: "These houses are too good. Probably have alarms, or servants. And they're rich and probably watch out for each other all the time" (p. 22). Likewise, an African-American burglar in our study, declared:

> *Man, I'd stand out in that neighborhood. What's a black man doing over here? That's what they'd be saying. They might think I was working somewhere, but they'd still keep a eye on me all the time I was around. When I'm out doing my thing, I like to be invisible. Man gotta fit in a place, then he be invisible. Can't be invisible in this neighborhood.*

The immediate risk cues considered by burglars in the target selection decision fell into three categories: visibility, occupancy, and accessibility.

Visibility

Visibility refers to the extent to which a house is overseen and observable by neighbors or passers-by. Visibility cues include the location of the house on the block; whether or not the windows and doors of the target site can be observed from neighbors' houses, and from the street. The visibility of a potential burglary target was considered by our informants as a primary factor in target selection. These cues provide answers to several questions of primary importance to the burglar. Are there neighbors present? Can the neighbors observe the target house from inside their homes? Can the neighbors entry into the target site be observed by passersby? Are there dogs that might bark and rouse neighbors? Are there shrubs, blind doorways, corners, or fences that will hide the burglar during entry? Is there traffic near the house that might see and report the burglar? Are there people in the neighborhood who watch the street and know who is and who is not at home?

The location and type of windows both at the target site and at neighbors' houses were considered critical by almost all informants. One burglar in our study stated: "Notice how that picture window looks out onto the street. The curtains stay open all the time and both the houses across the street can see straight into the living room. I wouldn't do [burglarize] this place."

Another said: "I'm looking at that upstairs window next door. You can see almost everything that goes on at this house from there. I'm worried about that window."

Wright and Decker also found that burglars considered visibility a major factor in their decision calculus. The burglars in their study preferred to enter from the rear of a house. They stated:

"I never [break in] through the front, unless I go through, like, a porch or something that could hide me. It's too obvious on the front. See, on the back it's not that obvious. The other . . . houses ain't facing the back. You don't find too many [potential onlookers] on the back, you mostly find them on the front."

Although the average burglar fears being seen, many professional burglars do not. Rather, they fear being seen *and reported.* The more experienced burglars stated that it was important to fit into a neighborhood or situation. They attempted to make their presence in a neighborhood seem normal and natural. The most professional of the burglars in our study, Robert, always drove a car that fit the neighborhood's socioeconomic level or a van disguised as a delivery vehicle. He dressed befitting the circumstances: as a plumber, delivery-eryman, or businessman. He would walk to the door of a potential target residence, open the screen door, and unobtrusively hold it open with his foot while he pretended to be having a conversation with a nonexistent person inside. He would then enter the house if the door was unlocked (he reported that many of his target houses were unlocked). If the door was locked, he pantomimed a conversation that appeared to instruct him to go around to the backyard. He would then walk around the house, sometimes stopping to gaze at some feature of the house or landscape, and take notes on a clipboard. When he got to the back yard, he entered the house from that point. To possible onlookers, he had knocked on the door, talked with the owner, and, following instructions, had gone to the rear of the house on some legitimate errand. Other times he would stop his car near a proposed target residence, open the hood, tinker around under the hood, appear to be angry, kick a tire, and angrily walk over to the potential target house. A neighbor or anyone else who might be watching saw only an angry man with a broken car, walking to a house to ask for assistance. Robert was not concerned about being seen. He expected to be seen, but because of his role-playing he did not expect to be reported (and he seldom was).

Visibility cues also include the extent of natural cover such as trees, shrubbery, and other landscaping. Houses with dense shrubbery near windows and doors were considered very vulnerable by the informants. One of the most important forms of cover was the privacy fence, a six- to eight-foot-high board or masonry fence enclosing a backyard. These fences were common in the area studied, and most informants considered them important in the target selection process. Some stated that they would not consider burglarizing a house that did not have a privacy fence. Although burglars were at risk while climbing the fence or entering through an unlocked gate, once inside, they were effectively protected from prying eyes by the fence. As one burglar stated: "Once I'm inside this fence, I can slow down and take my time. The place is mine."

Occupancy

The second category of risk cues are those that indicate *occupancy*. Occupancy cues include the presence of cars in the driveway or garage, visible residents, noise or voices emanating from the house, and other cues that indicate someone is at home. Research both before and after our study confirms the preference for unoccupied targets (Scarr; Reppetto; MacDonald, 1980; Bennett and Wright; Wright and Decker, 1994). Twenty-eight of the thirty burglars in our study stated that they would never purposely enter an occupied residence. Many reported that their greatest fear was that they would encounter the resident upon entering or that the resident would return home while they were still there.

The typical burglar is much more aware of our use of time than we are. As Rengert and Wasilchick (1985, p. 52) conclude, "We are all waiting to become victims of a burglar whose intuition about time coincides with our routine." Robert, a professional burglar in our sample revealed that he was not only aware of his victim's use of time, but also that of police and law enforcement: "You know when is the best time to do a burglary? Three o'clock in the afternoon. Mothers are picking up their kids at school and the police are doing shift change. Even if someone called the cops on me, they'd be in the middle of shift change and it would take longer to get here."

Our research confirmed that burglars work during periods when residences are left unguarded. They concluded that if a home is guarded (occupied) during the day, it is likely to be guarded by women. Rengert and Wasilchick (1985) stated that women who do not work outside the home tend to develop predictable patterns regarding the use of discretionary time for the purpose of shopping, errands, or visiting friends and relatives. Women who work outside the home develop similar patterns of time use on Saturday and Sunday. In either case, the use of discretionary time for the purpose of shopping and running errands is observable and predictable by residential burglars. Whenever the house is left unguarded, it is susceptible to burglary. They wrote, "When we combine the daily activities of many women, we can identify times when the typical house is not likely to be guarded" (Rengert and Wasilchick, 1985, p. 26). They found burglars to be most active between 10:00 and 11:00 A.M. and from 1:00 to 3:00 P.M.

The burglars in our study stated they preferred to work between 9:00 and 11:00 A.M. and in midafternoon. Most organized their working hours around school hours, particularly during the times when parents (usually mothers) took children to school and picked them up after school. Several told us that they waited "until the wife left to take the kids to school or go shopping." Most stated that they did not do burglaries on Saturday because people were usually home then. However, Sunday morning during church hours was considered prime time for weekend burglary.

Only a small number (n = 3) of burglars in our study committed residential burglaries at night. Most preferred to commit their crimes during daylight hours when they expected people to be at work and out of the home. As seen

Table 2.1 Day versus Night Burglary Ratings

Time	At Present (Now)	HYPOTHETICAL CIRCUMSTANCES	
		Assuming No One Is Home	Assuming No One Is Home and $250 Cash Is Inside
Day	3.52 (126)	4.97 (105)	5.88 (91)
Night	2.26 (117)	5.44 (108)	6.55 (107)
Rating[1]	$F_{(1,203)} = 11.36$	$F_{(1,173)} = 0.36$	$F_{(1,158)} = 2.00$
	$p < .05$	$p > .05$	$p > .05$

[1]The individual burglary attractiveness ratings (means) of burglars alone under the circumstances that actually prevailed at the time of the site inspection (now) and hypothetical circumstances for day and night. The number of individual ratings from which each mean was obtained is given in parentheses. The results of two-sample tests comparing day and night means are given below. The attractiveness scale ranged 1–10, with higher numbers indicating the residence was more attractive.

in Table 2.1, during a hypothetical exercise the informants rated targets more attractive and more vulnerable when they were rated during daylight hours than when the same targets were rated at night. However, the day versus night variation was not significant under the hypothetical circumstances in which the informants were asked to assume that no one was home, and to assume that no one was home and $250 in cash was inside. In the hypothetical situations the critical variable of occupancy was established (no one is home) and the variation across raters was essentially washed out. The lack of statistical significance under these circumstances is not, therefore, attributable to day versus night variations, but rather to the issue of occupancy.

Those who did commit nighttime burglary usually knew the victims and their schedules or took advantage of people being away from home in the evening during special events, such as high school football games. Pep squads at the high schools in the area studied decorate the front yards of the football team members with signs that identify the player, position, and uniform number. Burglars told us that they knew these houses would most likely be empty on Friday nights because the families attended the game. One said: "Man! Wait until football season. I clean up then. When they are at the game, I'm at their house."

Accessibility

Accessibility cues are those factors that indicate how easily the residence can be entered and how well the site is protected. These cues include location and type of doors and windows, as well as the extent of target hardening such as locks, burglar alarms, fences, walls, burglar bars, and dogs. Accessibility also includes neighborhood and street permeability. Houses on corners or on through-streets are more accessible than those on dead-end streets, cul-de-sacs, and other streets with few intersections. Houses in gated communities are much less susceptible than those open to all. Burglars generally agree

(Bennett and Wright; MacDonald, 1980; Taylor and Nee, 1988; Wright and Decker) that the critical elements in assessing vulnerability to break-in are:

- Larger, more expensive residences are more difficult to break-in to.
- Houses on cul-de-sacs, streets with few intersections, barricaded streets, and those in gated communities are among the least vulnerable to burglary.
- Alarm systems increase the risk.
- Burglar bars and good quality locks increase both the effort and the risk.
- Dogs increase the risk.

Large, Expensive Homes Although many burglars express a preference for burglarizing homes in the "rich" part of town, all agree that expensive homes are much more risky targets. Not only are burglars less likely to know the neighborhood and more likely to be noticed and identified as an outsider, they also recognize that homes in these areas have more security technology than smaller, less expensive homes. As one of our burglar subjects complained: "These people got solid wood doors and locks and alarms . . . maybe even laser guns protecting their house. It's just too hard. I don't mess with rich people's houses."

Complex Street Layouts, Barricaded Streets, and Gated Communities Accessibility also applies to the location of houses and other potential burglary targets. The more difficult the route to the prospective crime site, the less likely it will be targeted by the burglar. There has been a moderate amount of research on the susceptibility of houses on cul-de-sacs, less permeable streets, and those in gated communities to burglary and other forms of predatory crime. In a study of a residential area of Hartford, Connecticut, R. A. Gardiner (1978) demonstrated that closing off some streets to cars resulted in an overall decrease in crime. A study by James Lasley (1996) found a reduction in drive-by shootings in Los Angeles when some streets were closed to cars. Atlas and LeBlanc (1994) found a significant reduction in burglary in a south Florida community after implementation of street closures and barricades. Others (Bevis and Nutter, 1977; Beavon, 1984) have shown that the farther a residence is from main thoroughfares and arterial roads, the less likely it is to become a burglary target. The Brantinghams (1975) in a study of residential burglary in Tallahassee, Florida, found that burglary rates decreased sharply towards the core of residential areas.

A recent analysis of burglary in Greenwich, Connecticut, sought to determine the attributes of homes that attract burglars (Shachmurove, Fishman, and Hakin). The researchers obtained self-report data from 3,014 households, of which 339 had experienced burglary incidents. They found that homes closer to major arterial routes (providing escape opportunities for the burglars), corner homes, and those adjacent to wooded areas tended to have a greater probability of being burglarized.

Jesse, one of our experienced burglars, stated: "I don't like to go too deep [inside a neighborhood]. You get kinda lost once you get in those winding

streets and stuff. I like to stay close to the main road so I can find my way out and escape fast."

Roberto, a professional burglar in our sample, adamantly declared: "[I] don't do cul-de-sacs. Or dead-end streets. Always gotta have an escape route."

Burglar Alarms Burglar alarms can serve as occupancy proxies. As such, burglars try to avoid them (Wright and Decker). As one burglar told Wright and Decker (p. 96): "If I see an alarm out, like I say, they usually have them outside the house. I'll leave them alone automatically."

A major study of the effectiveness of burglar alarms was conducted by the Cedar Rapids, Iowa, police department. Matched pairs of 100 businesses and schools with previous burglaries were chosen for the experiment. One member of each pair was given a burglar alarm that sounded directly at the police station. The other half served as a control group. There was a reduction of 55 percent in attempted burglaries in sites with alarms compared to a reduction of only 8 percent for the control group (Rubenstein, Murray, Motoyama, and Rouse, 1980).

In their study of burglary in Greenwich, Connecticut, Shachmurove et al. (1997) concluded that "if the home is protected by an alarm the probability for a burglary is virtually nil" (p. 11). Our findings confirm these studies. One burglary subject advised: "Sometimes I pick a house to do and when I get up close I can see the wires taped to the window and I know they got an alarm. I just move on."

Another stated:

Most houses got a sign, like "This house protected by Westinghouse Security" or one of those other security companies. I just pass them by. People stupid to hit a house with an alarm system. Just go to one without it. That's common sense, you know. . . . Sometimes you see this blue sign that just says something like "This house protected by an electronic alarm system" without no company name on it. That's not real. . . . They just trying to scam you. You can get those signs at Radio Shack. Don't mean nothing.

Wright and Decker found that, "Most offenders . . . wanted to avoid alarms altogether and, upon encountering such devices, abandoned all thought of attacking the dwelling. Indeed, 56 of 86 subjects we questioned about this issue said that they were not prepared to burglarize an alarmed residence under *any* circumstances" (p. 125). One of their burglar subjects reported: "When I check the house out and be ready to get in it and I see an alarm, I'm ready to bust a window and I see that, I just back off it" (p. 126).

Although several burglars in our study boasted about disarming alarms, when pressed for details almost all admitted that they did not know how to accomplish that task. Two informants had disarmed alarm systems and were not particularly deterred by them. They stated that the presence of an alarm system gave them an additional cue as to the affluence of the residents, telling them that there was something worth protecting inside. One informant had

purposely taken a job installing alarm systems in order to learn to disarm them. Another informant stated that alarm systems did not deter her because she still had time to complete the burglary and escape before police or private security arrived in response to the alarm. She stated that she never took more than ten minutes to enter, search, and exit a house. She advised: "Police take fifteen to twenty minutes to respond to an alarm. Security [private security] sometimes gets there a little faster. I'm gone before any of them gets there."

Another professional burglar advised that he did not care whether a house had an alarm or not. He would go ahead and enter and begin to gather the goods he planned to steal. He said that after about five minutes the telephone would ring (the alarm company calling to verify the alarm). After the call, he stated that he had five to fifteen minutes before someone arrived.

In general, however, burglars agreed that alarms were a definite deterrent to their activities. Other factors being equal, they preferred to locate a target that did not have an alarm rather than to take the additional risk involved in attempting to burglarize a house with an alarm system. Over 90 percent of the informants would not choose a target with an alarm system. Most (about 75 percent) were deterred by a sign or window sticker that stated that the house was protected by an alarm system. As Richard, an experienced burglar, stated: "Why take a chance? There's lots of places without alarms. Maybe they're bluffing, maybe they ain't."

Locks, Burglar Bars, and Other Target Hardening Devices Past research has been inconsistent regarding the importance of locks on windows and doors. Scarr, and Rengert and Wasilchick (1985) found that burglars consider the type of lock installed at a prospective target site. Others (Bennett and Wright; Reppetto; Walsh, 1980) did not find locks to be a significant factor in the target selection process.

Early research evaluating "target hardening" techniques in four public housing projects in Seattle (1975) and in Chicago's Cabrini-Green public housing (1979) found that installation of deadbolt locks and other such techniques significantly reduced the burglary rate in those areas. From their review of these programs, Rubenstein et al. (1980) concluded that locks are a factor considered by burglars in target selection. Rengert and Wasilchick (1985) wrote: ". . . most of the burglars we interviewed are easily discouraged by a tough lock. With so many opportunities, many burglars will move on rather than struggle with a deadbolt lock" (p. 90).

In a recent study, Wright and Decker found that locks and windows and doors were usually not considered during the initial phase of the target selections process because they were not able to be seen from a distance. They wrote, "If locks were considered at all, this usually occurred at a later stage" (p. 98). Once a target was selected, the burglar would deal with the problem of locked doors and windows when the problem was actually encountered: "Locks play a part [in discouraging burglars], but . . . [if] you got the right tools, you could go up to the front door and open it as quickly and as easy as if you had your own key . . . " p. 120).

The majority of informants in our study initially stated that they were not deterred by locks, just as in the case of alarm systems. However, during burglary reconstructions, we discovered that given two potential target sites, all other factors being equal, burglars prefer not to deal with a deadbolt lock. After the burglar compared a few sites and discovered his or her own preference for doors without deadbolt locks, they were better able to evaluate their own preferences. A typical response to our questions about deadbolt locks was: "I gotta be in and out in two, three minutes. I ain't got time to mess with no tough lock."

Another of our subjects said: "I never really thought about it. I can bust open a deadbolt if I got time, but going back on it, I usually just find a house without one."

The variation in findings regarding security hardware appears to be related to the degree to which burglars are either rational or opportunistic. To the extent to which burglars are primarily opportunistic, locks appear to have some deterrent value. The opportunistic burglar chooses a target based upon its perceived vulnerability to burglary at a given time. Given a large number of potential targets, the burglar tends to select the most vulnerable of the target pool. A target with a good lock and fitted with other security hardware will usually not be perceived to be as vulnerable as one without those items. The rational, planning burglar chooses targets on the basis of factors other than situational vulnerability and conceives ways in which he or she can overcome impediments to the burglary (such as the target site being fitted with a high quality deadbolt lock). Thus, to the extent that burglars are rational planners, deadbolt locks have limited utility for crime prevention. Our findings, however, support the deterrent value of deadbolt locks; 75 percent of the burglaries reconstructed during our research were opportunistic offenses. Many of those burglaries would have been prevented (or displaced) by the presence of a quality deadbolt lock. It is important to note that nearly one half of the burglary sites in the present study were entered through open or unlocked windows and doors. The findings are very similar to those of Rengert and Wasilchick (1985), who found that burglary through unlocked doors was a "surprisingly frequent occurrence." They wrote:

Many burglars build their careers on the mistaken belief held by residents that "it can't happen here," or "I'll only be next door for a minute." More than one of the burglars we talked to burglarized open houses while the residents were in the back yard doing yard work.

Dogs   Almost all studies agree that dogs are an effective deterrent to burglary. Wright and Decker (p. 208) stated that few of the burglars in their study were prepared to tackle a house with a dog. Reppetto (1974) found that only about one-third of burglars under the age of twenty-five years reported that dogs would not be a deterrent. Although there is some individual variation among burglars, the general rule is to bypass a house with a dog—any dog. Large dogs represent a physical threat to the burglar and small ones are often noisy,

attracting attention to the burglar's activities. We found that although many burglars have developed contingency plans to deal with dogs (petting them, feeding them, or even killing them), most burglars prefer to avoid them. When asked what were considered absolute "no go" factors, most burglars responded that dogs were second only to occupancy.

Approximately 30 percent of the informants, however, initially discounted the presence of dogs as a deterrent. Yet, during ride alongs the sight or sound of a dog at a potential target site almost invariably resulted in a "no go" decision. As Richard said: "I don't mess with no dogs. If they got dogs I go someplace else." Debbie told us that she was concerned primarily with small dogs:

Big dogs don't bark much. I talk to them through the fence or door and get them excited. Then I open the gate or the door and when they charge out, I go in and shut the door behind me. They are outside and I'm in. Little dogs yap too much. They [neighbors] look to see what they are so excited about. I don't like little yapping dogs.

Some of the more professional burglars were less concerned with dogs and had developed techniques for dealing with them. In general, however, the presence of a dog was considered an effective deterrent.

SUMMARY

Burglary appears to be a highly rational crime, being committed almost exclusively to obtain money. While thrill, excitement, and revenge do play a minor role in the etiology of the offense, it is primarily young, inexperienced burglars who report such motives. Once the decision is made to commit a burglary, the burglars must select a likely target. We found that most of them employ a decision-making strategy that has four components. The burglar begins with an assumption that each proposed target site contains at least some minimal potential gain. He or she must then determine whether the target site might be occupied, and whether the site can be broken into readily. These determinations are made on the basis of evidence obtained from observing environmental cues at or near the target site and employing the mental template constructed through past experience and the recounted experiences of others.

Burglars use three categories of environmental cues to assess these risk factors: (1) cues that indicate the visibility of the proposed target site; (2) cues that indicate whether the target site is occupied; and (3) cues that indicate the degree of difficulty that might be expected in actually breaking into the site. The specific content of these cues has varied widely across prior studies.

We found that burglars are opportunistic and are easily deterred or displaced from one target site to another. Situational factors such as the presence of a dog, an alarm system, security hardware, and alert neighbors may be the most effective deterrents.

3

✦

The Burglary Event

O nce the burglar has selected a target, the problem of effecting entry, locating stealable items, and escaping with the stolen items arises.

These problems require the use of tactics to reduce the risk and make maximum use of the time and resources available. The tactics used are remarkable in their consistency across studies. This may be the result of simple common sense, or it may result from sharing of techniques by burglars on street corners, in bars, and in prisons and jails.

PROBING FOR OCCUPANCY

Since occupancy is such a critical component of the burglar's strategy, it is important that the burglar develop techniques to probe the potential target site to determine if anyone is at home. There are various ways, some quite ingenious, in which burglars probe the target to determine occupancy.

The most common probe used by our informants was to send one of the burglars, usually the most presentable (or the woman), to the door to knock or ring the doorbell. If someone answered, the prober would ask directions to a nearby address or for a nonexistent person, for example, "Is Ray home?" The prospective burglar would apologize and leave when told that he or she had the wrong address. Burglars also occasionally ring the doorbell and ask the resident for use of the phone: "My car broke down across the street. May I use your phone to call a garage?" This is a good strategy. If the resident refuses,

the prober can leave without arousing suspicion. If, however, the resident agrees, the prober has the additional opportunity to assess the quality and quantity of the potential take and to learn more about the security, location of windows and doors, dogs, alarms, and so forth. Several who used this strategy reported that they usually raised the hood of their car or removed a tire in order to give their story legitimacy. Rengert and Wasilchick (1985) reported similar strategies: "One of our burglars likes to pretend to have car problems. He would turn into a driveway of a likely house and raise the hood of his car. If the doorbell was answered, he asked for water for his overheated radiator" (p. 89).

Debbie, one of the female burglars in our study, used her two-year-old daughter in her occupancy probes. She would pretend to have car trouble in front of the prospective target house. She would ring the doorbell while holding the child. If someone answered the door, she asked to use the phone and to allow her to bring the child in out of the heat or cold, as the case might be. Most allowed her to come in. She would then have access to knowledge about the items in the home and sometimes other valuable information about security arrangements. She stated:

> *This one woman invited us in and gave us some water to drink. She just talked and talked. She was kinda old and I think she was lonesome or something. She started telling me all about her collection of silverware and tea services. She showed them off to me as we were sitting in her living room. She told me that she was worried about someone stealing them. While she was in the kitchen getting us a glass of cold water, I stole her keys that were sitting in a crystal bowl near the front door. Came back the next day and got her silver and a bunch more stuff too.*

Several informants reported obtaining the resident's name from the mailbox or from a sign over the door. They would then look up the telephone number and call the residence, leaving the phone ringing while they returned to the target home. If they could still hear the phone ringing when they arrived back at the house, they were sure that the house was unoccupied. This technique suggests that home owners should not place their name anywhere outside their home. This gives the burglar the information needed (name and address) to look up the telephone number.

Some burglars, particularly the more experienced and skilled, will probe neighbors next door to, and across the street from, the target. The ideal target is one where no one is home adjacent to and in houses overlooking the target. One burglar informant chose houses next door to homes that exhibited a "For Sale" sign. She would dress and act like a potential buyer, walking around the yard of the for-sale home, peering in windows, and so on, finally entering the backyard of the for-sale home and from there climbing the adjoining fence into the backyard of the target home. She told us:

> *One time I was walking around pretending to be looking at the "For Sale" house when a man came outside. I started to run but he invited me in to get a better look. He thought I was really someone wanting to buy his house. I got a really good tour of the place and I was coming back the next day to hit it, but I got arrested for*

something else that night and by the time I got out, the sign was gone. Someone bought it, I guess.

Some burglars watch a target home until they see the occupants leave for work in the morning. After a quick probe for a remaining occupant, they enter the house. Armando, a "retired" burglar in our study recalled his technique: "I used to drive around a neighborhood in the morning until I saw the woman leave home. Usually she was taking kids to school. Most times the man leaves first, going to work. Once the wife and kids leave, the house is empty."

One informant in the study dressed in jogging gear and removed a piece of mail from the potential target house mailbox. He then knocked on the door and if the resident answered, he told them he had found the piece of mail in the street and was returning it. He told us: "No one is suspicious of a jogger. Fact is, they think you're really honest when you give them the mail. Never get suspicious or anything."

The main concern of all the burglars was that they created no suspicion during their probes. Most had a good intuitive sense of how they need to act to appear "normal." The key, according to our subjects, is to be bold. As one told us: "You gotta go up to the place like you belong there. Like you own it. If you look scared or shy, they get suspicious right off. No matter what your story, it works if you act all normal." A burglar in Wright and Decker's (1994, p. 106) study mirrored these comments. He said:

"You don't want to go in a place thinking things that will upset you. You got to be natural, man; walk up to the house like it's yours. You got to look natural. [If the] police ride by, man, wave at 'em . . . You don't want to do nothing that draws suspicion; being nervous is how you get caught."

EFFECTING ENTRY

Once the decision is made to break in to a particular site, the burglar must use his or her skills to actually gain entry. There is a wide range of skill levels among burglars. Most burglars are not really skilled. They use brute force whenever possible. Techniques such as picking a lock or disarming an alarm system are beyond the ability of 99 percent of all burglars.

The break-in techniques, like the occupancy probes, were generally similar across studies. Although there were occasional unusual and creative methods, the skills appeared to be generic. Several studies have analyzed point of entry for burglars (Scarr, 1973; Reppetto, 1974; McDonald, 1980; Maguire, 1982; Wright and Decker, 1994). American studies tend to differ from those in Britain. For example, Maguire (1982) reported that the main point of entry in Britain was through windows (60 to 70 percent). On the other hand, American researchers have found doors to be the most common entry point by approximately the same percentage (60 to 70 percent). Our study revealed that rear or side doors were the most common entry point. Jerry's comment was typical: "I always go 'round the back. Most houses around here got six

foot wood fences in the back. Nobody can see you back there. Fronts are too dangerous. Anybody going by can see what you are doing." "The back of the house was also preferred by the burglars in Wright and Decker's study. As one burglar told them: "It's too obvious on the front. . . .You don't find too many [potential onlookers] on the back, you mostly find them on the front" (p. 121).

We found that burglars usually took advantage of unlocked windows and doors in about equal numbers. In one-fourth of the cases, our subjects reported entering through an unlocked door. Entering through an opened or unlocked attached garage and then into the house was a popular technique. The burglars told us that few people locked the door between the garage and the main house. Even when that door was locked, the burglar had time and privacy from inside the garage to break the lock and enter. Sometimes the garage contained the necessary tools to assist the break-in. One subject told us that when confronted with a locked door inside a garage, he found a prybar on a shelf immediately next to the door. "It was like they left me a key," he said.

Another 25 percent found an opened or unlocked window. Although breaking a window is relatively simple, many of our informants felt the noise caused by breaking glass was too risky. One told us: "People ignore lots of noises—bumps, bangs, and that kinda noise. But breaking glass gets attention. Almost anybody will look to see where a breaking glass noise comes from. I don't break windows if there is any other way [to get in]."

One of our informants, among the most skilled of all the subjects in the study, was employed for a period of time by a glass repair and replacement company. He could remove a pane of glass in less than a minute and replace it when he left. He stated: "I always put the pane back in and I don't disturb anything in the house. Sometimes the burglary doesn't even get reported. If I take small stuff, like jewelry, sometimes the people don't even miss it for a week or two and when they do, they think they lost it or something."

A popular way of entering a residence is through sliding glass patio doors. These doors may be popped out of their sliding tracks by hand or with the aid of a crowbar or screwdriver. Entry is quick and noiseless. Less skilled burglars insert a screwdriver between the door and the frame, break the usually cheaply built locks, and slide the door open. Some informants considered this method less professional than removing the door completely, although both appear to be quick and noiseless. Jerry, one of the more skilled burglars in our study, reported:

Those patio doors that most people have are better than a having a key; I can take one off the tracks in two seconds. Lot of people put a broomstick or a rod in the track so it can't slide open. That don't do any good 'cause I take 'em off top to bottom. Put my foot on the bottom part of the door and then push up with my feet and hands at the same time and off it comes.

Several burglars reported removing window air conditioning units and entering through the resulting opening. Another stated that he had removed skylights and entered through the roof. Three informants used large channel lock pliers to twist the doorknob off the front door of the residence. This

technique works so quickly on most doors that the burglar appears to be using a key to enter. One petite female burglar was able to crawl through pet doors. Her burglaries stumped law enforcement for a considerable period because there was no evidence of forced entry in her jobs. Another burglar put his three-year-old daughter through pet doors and other small openings. After gaining entry in this manner, she had been taught to open the back door of the house for her father.

Some burglars may simply kick down a door or smash a window with little apparent concern for noise. These are usually heroin addicts who are sick and in desperate need of a fix; cocaine, crack, or amphetamine users who are high; or the least experienced and non-skilled burglars. These measures subject the burglar to a much greater risk of detection and arrest.

THE SEARCH

Once inside a residence the burglar must search and locate stealable items. Few burglars make a careful search of the whole dwelling. They need to get in and get out as quickly as possible. Most told us that they did not want to be in the house more than two or three minutes. Almost all of our subjects stated that five minutes was their outside time limit. They believed that even if they were seen and reported, police response time would always be more than five minutes. Donna explained: "Usually people will take a few minutes, two or three minutes or even longer, to decide whether to call the police. Then it takes the police five or ten minutes to show up—unless the car just happens to be in the same area. . . . If you can get in and out in five minutes, you gonna be okay."

Once inside, the majority of our subjects (excepting the younger, less experienced ones) would first go to the side of the house they had not entered from and open a window or door as a possible escape route. As Donna told us: "If I go in the back door, I go to the front door and unlock it, so I can get out quick if I have to. Sometimes I open a window too. I don't want to be trapped if the law comes."

Almost all of our subjects reported that they first went to the master bedroom and bath. Here they expected to find jewelry, money, and sometimes guns. As Felson (1998) has shown, cash, jewelry, and other lightweight easily concealable items are the most sought-after by thieves. He writes, "Of central importance for becoming a target of predatory property crime is the value of the target proportional to its weight" (p. 60). Wright and Decker also found that the master bedroom was the first and primary search site:

With few exceptions . . . the interviewees were agreed that, upon entering a dwelling, one should make a beeline for the master bedroom, this is where cash, jewelry and guns are most likely to be found. (p. 142)

One of their subjects reported:

The first thing you always do when you get into a house is you always go to the bedroom. That's your first move . . . because that's where the majority of people

keep they stuff like jewelry or cash. You know it's gon be a jewelry box in the bedroom; you know you ain't gon find it in the living room. Guns, you ain't gon find too much in the living room." (p. 143)

Our subjects made similar observations. Burglars told us that bedroom closets and dressers were good places to find stashes of cash (and sometimes drugs). One said:

I always go to the master bedroom closet first. I look in shoe boxes and in the pockets of coats. People think that coat pockets are good places to hide things. Then I look under the mattress and in the bathroom. Most women keep their jewelry in the bathroom, so they can put it on in the morning easy. Sometimes it's in a jewelry box and sometimes just laying out on the counter. Dresser drawers sometimes have good stuff in 'em. Especially the top drawer and the bottom drawer.

Most of our subjects stated that they also looked in medicine cabinets. Here they were looking for prescription drugs such as pain killers, psychotropic drugs, and amphetamine-based products. Burglars also frequently look in the freezer section of the refrigerator for hidden cash. As one burglar asserted: "People think they pretty smart, putting money in the freezer. Cold cash, you know. I always look there."

Other popular items to steal are bottles of liquor, small color television sets, VCRs, stereos, compact discs, and DVD players, computers (especially laptops), and other electronic equipment. Some burglars will steal power tools from the garage.

Our subjects told us that when working in pairs or small groups, many burglars develop a division of labor in the search process. One subject who always worked with two "crime partners," stated: "When we get in, I go to the bedrooms and look for jewelry, money, and guns. One goes 'round unplugging the stereos and computers and stuff and the other one puts everything in a sheet or a pillowcase and takes it outside to the alley."

Others assign one of the burglars, usually the youngest and least experienced, as lookout. His or her job is to watch the windows and warn the others of someone returning home or a police car. Many reported that this had been their first assignment as a member of a burglary "crew":

When I was first coming up I always got the job of looking out. Sometimes I went in the house with the posse [burglary crew] and watched the street from the window. Sometimes I stayed outside and watched for people coming home or the police. Usually inside, though. After awhile, they let me do other stuff, like lookin' for money and stuff.

THE GETAWAY

Once inside the target dwelling and after locating items to steal and take away, the burglar must effect a safe getaway. Burglars are usually as concerned with stealth when leaving the burglary site as when entering. Most of our burglar subjects prepared their getaway even as they entered the dwelling.

Many opened a door or window opposite the entry site in order to effect a quick getaway if necessary. They wished to have at least two avenues of escape. They were especially concerned with two-story homes when searching for items to steal on the second floor. They felt that the stairs were their only reasonable exit and which trapped them in the house in case of an early return of the residents or should the police arrive. The subjects preferred to exit by means of a door—the back door whenever feasible. Windows were usually too small to allow television sets, microwave ovens, and computers to fit through.

Since most residential burglaries occur during daylight hours, leaving a residence loaded down with stolen items is problematic. The burglar is always anxious to convert the stolen items to cash. This is particularly true in the case of drug-using burglars, who frequently need money to purchase additional drugs. Thus, their preferred "loot" is cash. However, most burglaries result in the burglar obtaining jewelry, electronic devices, and other noncash items, which must be sold. Transporting these items from the crime site to where they can be sold is always risky. This is especially true for burglars who walk or ride bicycles to the crime site. As Mark observed:

You can't just walk down through the neighborhood carrying a television. I've done it but it ain't smart. I know this one dude that got run down by the guy whose house he just did. He tried to outrun him carrying a pillowcase full of silverware and stuff. What ya gotta do is hide the stuff and come back at night or have somebody with a car meet you in the alley.

While they often desperately needed the money that the stolen items would bring, most of the burglars we interviewed were rational enough to take precautions against being seen with the stolen items in broad daylight. One technique used by many involved taking the items they stole from a house out the back door, and secrete them in the alley, in or behind a garbage dumpster. They would then be free to leave the area with no evidence of the crime on them and to return at night to pick up the items.

A TYPOLOGY OF BURGLARS

Throughout the study, it was obvious that burglars exhibited wide variation in experience, skill, commitment to burglary, and the level of planning and forethought given to their crimes. One way to categorize them would be to the extent to which they were opportunists as opposed to being planners. Our subjects fell along a continuum between being passively opportunistic—that is, taking advantage of presented opportunities when they occurred randomly in the course of their routine activities—to seeking out and creating opportunities for crime. However, an opportunistic burglar was not necessarily an amateur. Opportunism does not necessarily imply lack of rationality. A

burglar may make a completely rational decision to take advantage of certain criminal opportunities when they arise, or to seek out or even create opportunities in a systematic manner.

Bennett and Wright identified three categories of burglars: planners, searchers, and opportunists. The *planner* selects a target well in advance of the offense; the *searcher* reconnoiters an area seeking out a suitable target; and the *opportunist* responds "there and then" to an attractive set of environmental cues, for example, an open garage door at a site that is apparently unoccupied at the precise time the potential burglar arrives on the scene. They concluded that only 7 percent of their sample of 117 burglars were opportunists. They found it "surprising that so few offenders mentioned committing opportunistic crimes" (p. 44), and suggested that limited definition of "opportunistic" and the age and experience level of their sample might account for the small number of opportunistic burglars.

We chose a broader definition of opportunist, one that incorporated two of Bennett and Wright's categories: searcher and opportunist. The searcher takes advantage of sought-out opportunities and the opportunist responds to presented opportunities. We considered burglars in both categories to be opportunists. The opportunist may commit the burglary immediately after searching the target or may wait until the situation is more advantageous for the commission of a criminal act. Bennett and Wright delineated between the searcher and opportunist categories on the basis of the elapsed time between perception of the criminal opportunity and commission of the crime. The searcher allowed time to pass between locating a target and committing the burglary (presumably for planning purposes, whereas the opportunist committed the burglary there and then). With the exception of very inexperienced juveniles, few burglars (and none in our sample) fit the Bennett and Wright definition of opportunist. Whether or not a burglar waits and plans after site selection appears to be determined more by the immediate situation than by his or her orientation as opportunistic or planner (or irrational versus rational).

Opportunism then, by our definition, turns on the target selection process, *not on the time between* selection and commission of the burglary. A rational process might well necessitate taking advantage there and then of a particular juxtaposition of situational factors. For example, while reconstructing a past burglary, Ramon stated: "I saw this place one day when I was cruising looking for a place to hit. It looked perfect, but it was too big to do alone. I needed a posse [gang of burglars]. I got me three other dudes and went back about a week later and did it."

He explained that the house appealed to him because of the apparent affluence of the residents, the secluded location of the house on the lot, and an unlocked garage door. However, the house was very large and could be approached from several directions. He feared that without lookouts and extra persons to search once inside, the risk would be too great. His decision to burglarize the site was an opportunistic one, although his process was that of a planner. Several other prior burglaries reconstructed by the same individual were purely opportunistic. In one instance, he "happened by" a vulnerable target

while on his way home from a party. The site was vulnerable right then. He committed the burglary with no further planning than to probe briefly to determine whether the house was occupied. Although unquestionably opportunistic, the burglary was nonetheless rational: the site was unoccupied, a window was open, and the neighborhood appeared to be deserted. He could not have expected to find a more advantageous set of circumstances than those that were presented there and then.

Exploiting opportunity characterized the target selection processes in over 75 percent of the burglaries reconstructed during our research. Even the very experienced and highly skilled burglars among our informants often took advantage of presented opportunities when they arose. Chance opportunities occasionally presented themselves while the professional was casing and probing potential burglary targets chosen by more rational means. When these opportunities arose, the professional burglar was as likely as other burglars to take advantage of the situation.

Because opportunity appeared to characterize almost all of the burglars at some level or another, we chose to consider opportunity as only one of several variables in creating a typology of burglars. We identified three types of burglar: the *novice*, the *journeyman*, and the *professional*.

The novice is at the beginning of his or her career as a burglar or a juvenile who commits one or more burglaries and then desists. The novice frequently learns from older, more experienced burglars in the same neighborhood. These older burglars are often relatives, frequently older siblings. The novice is usually initially allowed to go along with the older burglars, acting as the "lookout" for the older youth. As the novice learns the techniques of burglary, he or she may become a permanent member of the older group of burglars or may take the knowledge gained from the older group back to his or her own peer group and begin committing burglaries with the younger group without continued supervision from the older burglars.

A major determinant of whether the novice stays with the older group or returns to his or her own age cohort is whether he or she can locate and develop a market for the property obtained from burglaries. Older mentors, who teach novices the techniques of burglary, often conceal the identity of their fences. Until younger burglars can find a regular market for their stolen property, they have to depend on the older burglar. Even when they go out on their own they must rely on their mentors to sell the property for them (and pay a fee or a percentage of the gains). Once the market is established, however, the novice may advance along the continuum toward the journeyman level. Four of the informants in the present study were novice burglars.

Once an individual has mastered the technical and organizational skills, made the requisite contacts for marketing stolen property, and developed what Sutherland (1937) called a "larceny sense," he or she may be considered a journeyman burglar. The journeyman category corresponds roughly to Shover's (1971) "serious thief." Journeymen are experienced, reliable burglars. The burglary style of the journeyman burglar is marked by a preference for searching out or creating opportunities, much like the searcher category identified by

Bennett and Wright, and the suburban burglar studied by Rengert and Wasilchick (1985). Rather than waiting for criminal opportunities to present themselves during ordinary daily activities, the journeyman searches out or creates opportunities. Selecting a community or neighborhood in which he or she feels comfortable, the burglar cruises around looking for a target site that looks vulnerable. The burglar may plan the act by casing the site for a period of a few hours to several days to assess the ease or difficulty of access and egress. Assistance in the form of additional persons may be necessary and the burglar may require time to put a team together. He or she may also determine that the situation and circumstances make a there-and-then hit advantageous and commit the crime immediately after target selection. In our study, twenty-one of the informants were classified as journeymen.

Professional burglars constitute the elite of the burglary world. They are differentiated from the other categories by the level of their technical skill, their organizational abilities, and the status accorded them by peers and generally by law enforcement authorities. Professionals do no usually commit crimes of opportunity. They plan and execute their crimes with deliberation. They have excellent contacts for disposing of stolen merchandise. They may or may not be drug addicts. Drug addiction does not preclude the designation *professional*. The primary difference between the professional and the journeyman burglar is the status accorded to each. Their status is recognized and accepted by others (other thieves, law enforcement, fences, etc.), and they are accorded "respect" befitting that status. Five of the informants in our study were considered professional burglars.

SUMMARY

Burglars must develop skills that include breaking and entering, searching for stealable items once inside a residence, escaping without detection or apprehension, and finally, disposing of the stolen items. These skills are usually learned from older more experienced "mentors," often members of the youth's family—older brothers or cousins. As time passes and the individual gains experience and develops skills, he or she may be accorded greater status as a burglar and gain access to fences and others who may assist in converting the stolen goods to cash. The extent and level of these skills, and the organizational ability they possess, along with the status accorded them by other burglars, determines whether they are considered a novice, a journeyman, or a professional burglar.

4

❖

Drug and Group
Effects on Burglars'
Decision Making

One of the weaknesses of much research employing a rational choice model is the failure to consider the lifestyles and daily activities of offenders (Wright and Decker, 1994). Research has consistently shown that a large proportion of property offenders are addicted to drugs or have used illegal drugs in the recent past (National Institute of Justice, 2000; Bureau of Justice Statistics, 1988; Johnson et al., 1985; National Institute of Justice, 1989b; Maguire and Pastore, 1999). If drug usage affects the generally rational decision model of target selection by residential burglars, and if a substantial proportion of burglars are drug abusers, decision-making models that assume a rational cognitive state are limited in what they can explain, how well they predict behavior, and how generally they apply. One of the purposes of our research was to determine how drug use affects burglary target selection and other decision-making processes of residential burglars, with particular emphasis on the influence of drugs on the rational decision model.

We also wished to discover the influence of the presence of co-offenders on the decision-making process. Some previous literature suggests that group decisions differ from individual decisions in very significant ways (Zajonc, 1965, 1980; Pruitt, 1971; Myers and Lamm, 1976; Shaw, 1981). Do group decisions tend to be riskier decisions, as some have suggested, or might they become more cautious? Are burglars who work with partners apprehended more often than those who work alone? Do burglars who work with partners have a higher rate of offending? Do drug effects interact with group effects? How do these issues influence the rational decision-making model?

PREVALENCE OF DRUG-USING BURGLARS

Our findings suggest that the percentage of drug-using burglars is much greater than that reported in prior studies. During our first session with the burglar informants, about one-half admitted to regular illicit drug use. As we developed rapport and trust with the informants, however, or when we confronted an informant whom we believed to be misrepresenting his or her drug use, we found that all of the informants were either drug addicts or regular users of illegal drugs. Because previous research (Åkerström, 1983; Bennett and Wright; Reppetto, 1974) has reported a much smaller percentage (30 to 60 percent) of drug users in burglar populations, we were concerned initially that our sample was biased in favor of drug users. Consequently, we attempted to actively recruit non-drug-using burglars. Both our informants and local law enforcement officials, however, advised us that there were virtually no burglars in the area who were not drug users. Although this finding could be an artifact of the sampling procedure or of the geographic locale where the study was conducted, alternatively it suggests that early research using incarcerated burglars as informants may have underestimated the prevalence of drug use among burglars. Previous studies have relied on incarcerated burglars or burglars on probation or parole as informants. The interviews were usually not conducted over a long period of time and the researchers did not have the opportunity to interact with the informants for a period of time sufficient to develop rapport and trust. There is little reason to believe that informants are completely truthful with researchers during one or two interviews conducted in circumstances that might appear threatening (in prison, probation offices, etc.). Studies involving free, active burglars tend to show a much higher concentration of drug-using burglars. In a recent study by Wright and Decker, fifty-nine of ninety-five burglars (62 percent) admitted using the proceeds from their burglaries on the purchase of drugs. Shover (1996, p. 93) argues that to better understand the choices made by persistent offenders, it is useful to examine the worlds in which much of their time is spent. He found that drugs and alcohol were an integral part of the lifestyles of the burglars and thieves he studied.

Our informants were contacted outside criminal justice channels, yet one-half of them initially denied drug use. Their subsequent admission to drug use came only after the third or fourth interview, and then sometimes only after being confronted about inconsistencies in their story.

INTERDEPENDENCE OF DRUGS AND CRIME

Our findings reveal an interdependence between drug abuse and residential burglary. This does not, however, imply that drug use is implicated in the etiology of burglary. In fact, most of our informants committed their first burglary before they began regular drug use (see also Faupel, 1987; Faupel and

Klockars, 1987). Once they began to use drugs regularly, however, they usually began to rely, at least partially, on criminal activity to maintain the habit. As their drug use intensified, the users (particularly heroin addicts) found regular employment increasingly difficult to maintain, and they often dropped out of legitimate society and into a drug-using, criminal subculture. Thereafter, most maintained their drug habit through full-time criminal activity. Because drug users must establish and maintain illicit contacts in order to buy drugs, they are drawn further into a network of criminal associates, and thus more deeply into a deviant lifestyle.

Developmental Processes of Drug Use and Burglary

The typical pattern of entry into the life-style of burglary and drug abuse among our informants was as follows:

1. At about age ten to thirteen, adolescents in a generally criminogenic environment were allowed to join a group of older (fourteen to seventeen) adolescents who either shoplifted or committed a burglary. This crime was usually committed in the neighborhood in which they all lived. The younger members were allowed to share in the proceeds, although they almost never received an equal share. If the property stolen was cash or later converted to cash, they bought candy, cigarettes, video game tokens, and so forth with their share. More frequently the younger members of the group were allowed to keep small items such as radios, boom-boxes, or toys. They used these items or traded them for other items.

2. This activity typically occurred three to ten times before the younger apprentices either progressed to doing a burglary more or less on their own or they became accepted as a more integral part of the older group. If they formed their own burglary crew (usually in groups of two or three), the first burglary on their own frequently resulted in a small amount of stolen property that they could not easily convert to cash because of lack of contacts to fence the goods. They kept the items or agreed to share their proceeds with an older, more experienced burglar in exchange for marketing the stolen property.

3. At this point, typically from one to six months after the first burglary with the older adolescents, they often began to buy alcohol, pills, or marijuana with some of the proceeds, or to trade the stolen property for drugs and alcohol.

4. As they grew more confident and gained more experience (and criminal associates), they located an outlet for their stolen goods—a local fence or a middleman to act as a go-between in disposing of the stolen property. In this manner they found themselves on the fringe of a delinquent/drug-using subculture. Drugs were now readily available and the youths now had money to purchase them.

5. The adolescents found that drugs and burglary facilitated each other. Smoking marijuana, crack cocaine, or drinking alcohol made the burglaries easier by reducing fear and inhibitions. Thereafter, burglaries were frequently committed under the influence of drugs and the proceeds were used to buy (or barter for) more drugs.

6. The focus of activity among the adolescents then changed from a focal concern with the excitement and thrills (Miller, 1958) and peer approval that came with committing burglaries to the use and abuse of drugs and alcohol. Burglary and other property crime became only a means of achieving the wherewithal to buy drugs. In a sense, the two activities could no longer be separated. They were two sides of the same coin, having evolved together in the adolescents' immediate past history.

When questioned as to whether they would be committing burglaries if they were not using drugs, virtually all of the informants stated they would not, or that their rate of offending would be much lower. Reppetto concluded that if drug abuse were cured or if drug addicts had their habits met in some way that did not require them to steal, "a major drop in Boston residential burglary rates would ensue" (p. 72). We agree that some types of criminal activity might be reduced; however, most of our informants also cited the excitement of the crime itself, the need for money to maintain a "fast life," and the independence of a life of crime as additional motivations for their burglaries. Shover (1996) has emphasized the concept of "life as party" for many, if not most of those who engage in drug use and crime. He writes:

A substantial proportion of the money earned by thieves is consumed by the high cost of drugs, but some is also used for ostentatious consumption and enjoyment of luxury items and activities that probably would be unattainable on the returns from the minimum wage jobs that increasingly characterize working-class employment. (p. 94)

THE RATIONAL DRUG ABUSER

Preble and Casey (1969) were the first to challenge the traditional image of the addict–criminal as an irrational "dope fiend." Their study of heroin addicts in New York City presented a view of the addict as a hard-driving career person whom they compared to a business executive. Our findings, as well as other recent research, support this characterization of the heroin addict (Faupel, 1987; Faupel and Klockars, 1987; Inciardi, 1979; Johnson et al., 1985). We believe that the addict might best be viewed as an entrepreneur who must be skilled and dedicated in order to survive. Unlike stereotypical dope fiends, the heroin addicts we interviewed approached burglary as an occupation, invariably referring to their crimes as work (see also Letkemann, 1973). Rico, a heroin addict, said: "I think of this as work just like you think of your job as work. You are a professor, I'm a junkie and a burglar."

Debbie, a female heroin addict, stated: "I get up every morning and go to 'work.' Before I comb my hair or brush my teeth, I go out and steal something

to get $20 for a fix. After I've fixed for the first time, I clean up and go to work again."

She explained that when she had failed to hold back some heroin from the night before, her first crime of the day was often unplanned and sometimes even desperate. "I steal anything," she said, "tools from the back of a truck or I break into a car and take something. It doesn't make much difference what it is or how dangerous it is. I need that first fix real bad." After her first fix, however, her crimes—usually burglaries—had a certain elegance in their planning and execution. She was proud of her work and the fact that, although she had been stealing daily for eight years, she had been arrested only twice and convicted only once. She received probation for that conviction because she was a first offender.

Controlling the Habit

The ability of heroin addicts to manage and regulate their addiction has been reported in several studies. Bruce Johnson and his associates (Johnson, Goldstein, and Dudraine, 1979) found that most heroin addicts do not take heroin every day. They also reported considerable variation in daily dosages. Stimson and Oppenheimer (1975) reported that two-thirds of a sample of London heroin addicts had abstained for a period of one week or more since they became addicted. Bennett (1986) found that many of the subjects in his study reported periods of abstinence lasting months or years, and that their daily consumption of heroin varied greatly: "Daily consumption was often variable, and addicts often voluntarily abstained for one or more days to manage their patterns of consumption" (p. 97).

We arrived at similar conclusions. On one occasion during our study, a police drug raid jailed almost every heroin dealer in an area of town where several of our addict-burglars usually "scored." For three days they were forced to search for alternative supplies and to buy from dealers they did not know and who did not know them. During this period, one informant with a $300 daily habit simply reduced his intake to "two papers" per day—about $40 in heroin. Others did the same. They did not appear to suffer significant physiological withdrawal symptoms during the short hiatus. We found that the most experienced drug users suffered the least. Although the more experienced addicts normally consumed a greater amount of drugs daily, they appeared to handle the drug shortage crisis better. They reported less sickness and fewer symptoms of withdrawal. One informant stated: "It's no big thing. It takes about three days before you get really sick. My bones hurt a little and I feel like I'm getting the flu. I can handle it."

He explained that he had suffered withdrawal many times and that the physiological symptoms were not as great as he had been told to expect when he was younger and less experienced. He said: "The first time you expect to get really, really sick. You always heard it was like dying. Since you expect it to be really bad, it is."

Other experienced addicts reported a similar ability to abstain or to reduce their dosage without severe physiological consequences. The consensus among

the older, more experienced addicts is that withdrawal, although unpleasant, is not as painful an experience as most believe. Most told us that the more severe symptoms of withdrawal do not begin until approximately three days after cessation of use. The experienced addict does not panic into premature withdrawal symptoms. One female addict illustrated this point, stating: "I used to think if I missed getting a fix I'd get sick. If I woke up and didn't have a fix I'd start withdrawing. Get chills and diarrhea. Now I know it was mostly in my mind. I don't like to, but I can go two or three days without getting really sick."

It appears, then, that the pains of withdrawal from heroin are at least partially driven by psychological expectations. Addicts who have had considerable experience with withdrawal can better handle the physiological consequences than those with less experience. From these findings, the heroin addict-burglar appears to be more rational and more capable of self-regulation than previously thought. Under most circumstances the heroin addict's crimes are as rationally conceived and executed as those of a non-drug-user with the same level of expertise.

The Cocaine-Using Burglar

Cocaine users (in powder or crack form) exhibited less ability to control their intake than did the heroin users we interviewed. Although it appeared that most cocaine users could skip days or even weeks between periods of cocaine use, once they began to use the drug they experienced a definite loss of control over their intake. Unlike heroin, which satiates the user after an appropriate dose, cocaine use results in a craving for more. The cocaine user is never satisfied (this is true to a lesser extent of the amphetamine user). Cocaine users frequently commit burglaries while under the influence of this stimulant drug, usually in order to buy more cocaine to satisfy the endless craving. Their crimes are frequently crimes of random opportunity and are often committed in a "smash and grab" manner. Cocaine users will not usually invest the time in planning and executing a burglary and are often not as subtle in gaining entry. They will kick down doors or break windows when less violent (and less noisy) alternatives are available. Cocaine and speed (methamphetamine) users are more prone to trash a house searching for property to steal. They will dump drawers and turn over mattresses in their haste. A burglary site that has been entered by kicking open the door or by smashing a window and then trashed by the burglar during the search for valuable items to steal is predictably the work of a burglar using a stimulant (cocaine or amphetamine) or of juveniles.

DRUG EFFECTS ON BURGLARY

One interesting finding regarding drugs was unexpected and, although reported previously (Bennett and Wright; Shover, 1971), had not been widely discussed or analyzed. We expected to find that burglars committed burglaries to buy drugs. We had not expected to find that burglars also used drugs to initiate

and facilitate the commission of their burglaries. Twenty-eight informants stated that, when possible, they fixed or "got high" before entering a target site. They referred to the need to "be steady," or to "keep up my nerve." Most concluded that they were better burglars when under the moderate influence of drugs or alcohol. Some reported enhanced vision and more acute hearing while under the influence of marijuana. Others perceived themselves to be more efficient, to act faster and with more decisiveness, while using cocaine. A larger group, over one-half of the informants, reported that they drank alcohol, fixed, or smoked marijuana to overcome the fear brought on by the act of entering the target site. The drugs used to deal with fear were primarily central nervous system depressants. With only two exceptions, even the informants whose regular drug of choice was a stimulant, such as cocaine or speed (methamphetamine), used depressant drugs immediately before a burglary to lower anxiety and reduce fear, thus facilitating the criminal event. Many stated that without drugs or alcohol they would not have the courage to initiate the act or to stay in the residence long enough to search for and locate the items to steal. Further, they believed that without a calming drug they tended to overlook important environmental cues related to risk, as well as items hidden in the house that they otherwise would find.

In recent years several studies have reported similar findings. Wright and Decker found that many of the burglars in their study utilized drugs to reduce anxiety or fear before committing the crime. One of their burglar subjects revealed: "I smoke [crack cocaine]. If I went [to do a burglary] straight, I wouldn't have the balls to do it" (p. 105).

David Indermaur (1995) in a study of Australian property offenders, also found that many reported using drugs and alcohol to obtain the necessary courage to commit the crime, stating that ". . . offenders may often get drunk to do a crime rather than do a crime because they are drunk" (p. 57).

Drugs and Emotional Arousal

Research on the effect of emotion on cue utilization suggests that emotional arousal acts to reduce the range of cues that an organism responds to and that performance is either improved or impaired depending on the nature of the task involved. The range of cue utilization is the total number of environmental cues that an organism observes and to which it responds (Easterbrook, 1959). As the level of arousal is increased, cue utilization is decreased. Emotional arousal increases, when experiencing general excitement, when under stress, or in threatening situations. Zajonc (1965, 1980) found that for individuals with high levels of arousal, responses to central cues were enhanced and more concentrated or focused, whereas responses to peripheral cues were impaired. Consequently, one might expect an increased ability to perform more auto-matic behavior patterns in high states of arousal when some task-irrelevant cues are neglected. However, such dominant responses may be inappropriate for situations requiring more creativeness and spontaneity, resulting in impaired performance. He described the phenomenon as a "funneling of the field of

awareness." Reduction of the perceptual field, as caused by fear and excitement or the physiological stress of drug withdrawal, might therefore restrict attention to only the more salient cues. To the burglar, then, whose task is complex, a highly aroused state (anxiety, fear, stress) would be counterproductive, because to enter a residence, search for and seize property, and leave undetected, he or she must attend to even the most subtle environmental cues. Burglars must concurrently attend and respond to stimuli and events both inside and outside the burglary site, and to the movements and actions of accomplices, neighbors, passersby, and occupants. This type of attention requires what is referred to as parallel processing. Air traffic controllers, pilots, and short-order cooks, as well as burglars, must possess parallel processing skills.

Wayne, an experienced burglar, stated that he always smoked marijuana before entering a target site "to reduce the paranoia" and to increase his awareness. He stated: "I'm scared to death to go in a house. If I didn't smoke a joint or have a few drinks I couldn't do it. If you get inside and you're not 'cool,' I mean if you're not aware of what's going on around you, you're gonna get caught."

Debbie, a heroin addict, stated that she fixed whenever possible before doing a burglary: "I'm so scared I can't think straight without some 'junk' or at least, some 'weed.' Once I've got straight, then I'm okay. I'm not afraid and I can think good enough to get the job done and get away safe."

Jamie, a heavy cocaine user, stated he would never use cocaine before doing a burglary: "Coke makes you paranoid, man. If you're scared, then you don't need to get paranoid too. You get to running around on the inside of the house and you can't think right and you miss a lot of stuff."

By using depressant drugs or alcohol at an appropriate dose and time before entering a target site, the burglar may reduce the level of arousal brought on by fear and thereby possibly increase the range of cues utilized. To this extent, he or she may actually become a better burglar. There is, however, an optimal level of arousal for a task, and reducing or increasing the level of arousal below or above an optimal point may impair rather than increase performance (the classic inverted U-shaped dose-response performance curve). The burglar who reduces arousal to the point of nodding off, or the cocaine or methamphetamine user who attempts to ward off fear by using a stimulant such as cocaine or speed, impairs his or her utilization of both central and peripheral cues, and impairs rather than facilitates performance. Billy, a burglar who used marijuana and alcohol heavily, reported: "One time, man, I smoked some dope before I went in this place. I was already about half drunk. I found this comic book inside one of the kids' bedrooms and started reading it. I must have gone to sleep, man, 'cause the next thing I remember this cop was standing there shaking me and telling me to wake up."

Drugs and State-Dependent Learning

Drug-induced state-dependent learning is now a well-established phenomenon, and has attracted considerable interest in the past twenty years, particularly when humans perform complex tasks under the influence of drugs.

State-dependent learning (SDL) refers to superior memory for information that is retrieved in the same state as when it was learned. Early SDL studies were conducted using animals after Overton (1964) found that when rats initially learned tasks under the influence of pentobarbital, their initial learning may not transfer to the nondrug state. On the other hand, the initial learning could be reactivated when the rats were administered pentobarbital again. SDL has received considerable attention since the 1960s and has been demonstrated in the laboratory using human and animal participants with a variety of drugs (Jarbe, 1986; Lowe, 1986). In the late 1970s, state-dependency effects had also been demonstrated as a function of emotional state and physiological arousal (Eich, 1989). For example, information and behaviors associated with a particular emotion and context in the past will be more accessible under fear and the fear-arousing context. Such examples of state-dependency have been referred to as *state-dependent memory (SDM)*.

There are some rather intriguing implications for burglary by extrapolating state-dependent phenomenon from the laboratory to real-world burglars. One implication is that burglars who repeatedly break into houses under the influence of a specific drug are developing a set of responses, memories, and reasoning abilities that are best retrieved under similar conditions, i.e., subsequent use of the same drug in the burglary context. As mentioned before, most of the subjects in our study sample concluded that they were better burglars when under the moderate influence of drugs. Conversely, burglary skills learned and performed in the drug state may not transfer to a subsequent burglary performed when drug free. Simply stated, the use of the same drug during burglary serves likely to aid in the recall of technique and the retrieval of information relative to burglary, and inconsistency in drug use during burglary may lead to forgetfulness, inefficiency, or carelessness. For example, consider the burglar who consistently carries out burglaries under the influence of cocaine. Although hardly a smooth professional with cocaine, one could speculate that if he or she were to engage in a burglary while drug free, or with a depressant drug, performance would be even less efficient. While speculative, this may account for the high rate of apprehension on the part of cocaine-using burglars—they were not consistently on cocaine when they conducted their burglaries.

It is also conceivable that for the burglar who learned burglary technique, information, and reasoning under the influence of drugs to not only use drugs before each subsequent burglary to gain better access to such knowledge and skills while high, but also to dissociate himself from other thoughts or feelings learned while drug free which might have interfering qualities, e.g., fear of being seen, fear of an unexpected householder, and apprehension or harm (Lang, Craske, Brown, and Ghaneian, 2001). Thus, inhibition of fear-provoking information, often cited by our burglars as an important reason for using drugs before burglary, may be explained, in part, as a product of the state-dependent phenomenon. Namely, it seems reasonable to assume that fears of incarceration and so forth were learned in the drug-free state, and that such fears would not transfer to the cognitive state of the burglar if high while executing the next burglary.

Reinforcement

Using drugs before entering a target site not only reduces fear, increases utilization of environmental cues, and facilitates the recall of knowledge and skills learned in burglaries, it also reinforces the burglary behavior (Akers, 1985, 1997). Years of studies associated with the principles of learning have consistently demonstrated that behaviors that are followed by reward are more likely to recur than behaviors that go unrewarded. Burglary is rewarding (or reinforcing) in many ways.

Many of our burglar subjects reported that the planning and target selection process was a rewarding experience for them. Just as many persons enjoy planning a vacation or a fishing or hunting trip, many burglars reported that planning a burglary was a pleasurable experience. Searching for a suitable target was also considered rewarding by most of our informants. For many, the search was a social activity accompanied by drinking and drug taking. Rengert and Wasilchick (1985) reported similar findings. They described one informant's activities in the target search: "It was almost a game. . . . They enjoyed viewing the houses and almost made a game of predicting if anyone was home in the houses with desirable attributes of wealth" (pp. 37–38).

The actual break-in also has reinforcing characteristics. The informants almost unanimously reported a "rush" upon entering the site. Some referred to the feeling as a "rush of adrenaline." All found the feeling very pleasurable. The searching of the burglarized residence for items to steal was considered pleasurable by all of our informants. Almost all of them described the feeling as one of excitement and anticipation. Several described the feeling with a statement similar to that of George: "I know that once I'm inside, everything I can find is mine. I can have anything there. It's like Christmas."

A successful burglary also provides the participants with cash and/or property that can be converted to cash (or drugs). This is a powerful positive reinforcement.

The burglar is also rewarded through camaraderie with co-offenders after the successful crime. Just as golfers often replay the match afterward in the clubhouse, burglars frequently reported partying following a successful burglary, everyone retelling their own version of the activity. Such recapping of the behavior that precedes it (Spiegler and Guevremont, 2003) Fear and anxiety, for example, are unpleasant states with internal physiological correlates (increased heart rate, blood pressure, perspiration, and so forth). The reduction of fear and anxiety associated with drug use before the burglary serves simply to reinforce drug use (because it reduced or eliminated the fear) and thereby increases the likelihood that drug use will be used prior to the next burglary.

Reinforcement can also occur when unpleasant situations or states are reduced. This is termed negative reinforcement. Many people, including professionals, mistakenly equate the term negative reinforcement with punishment. Reinforcement, whether positive or negative, always refers to the strengthening of the behavior, whether positive or negative, always refers to the strengthening behavior is often accompanied by the use of alcohol and drugs, further reinforcing the behavior.

With both positive and negative reinforcers at work, and because burglary is among the crimes with the lowest clearance rates (little systematic punishment that might inhibit the behavior), the behavior tends to perpetuate itself.

Target site selection, as opposed to the actual burglary, was just as often accomplished by our informants without specific benefit of drugs. This finding does not contradict the conclusion that using drugs may facilitate memory, parallel processing, and decision making while in the actual act of burglary; in fact, it complements findings on use of drugs prior to burglary to reduce fear. Selecting the target does not typically involve fear, stress, or other emotions that increase arousal and narrow perceptual awareness because the burglar is usually not at risk during the process. However, when burglars work in groups—with partners—even during site selection when they are not at risk, many report an increase in arousal. They refer to this arousal as "psyching each other up." Drug use may reduce this arousal produced by the presence of others and enhance the target selection decision process. On the other hand, using drugs during the target selection stage when working alone could conceivably impair decision making. When little or no fear intrudes on the decision process, drug usage may produce a rebound effect and reduce utilization of both central and peripheral cues. This was illustrated during a ride-along session with two informants, Ramon and Jesse, who usually worked together and who, when stable, were almost always in agreement about the vulnerability or potential risk of a target site. During this session, however, Ramon was very high on cocaine and Jesse was completely stable. Ramon rated each site considerably more vulnerable and much less risky than did Jesse. Ramon apparently did not consider (or perceive) a large, unfriendly dog in one yard, obvious signs of occupancy at another site, and neighbors outside next door to another site. One week later, when both Ramon and Jesse were stable and essentially equivalent in their intoxication, their burglary attractiveness ratings on the same sites coincided almost exactly. Clearly, state-dependency phenomena and the fear reduction properties of drugs are worthy of further exploration in the real world of burglary in particular, and criminal behavior in general.

Drug Effects on Burglary Attractiveness Ratings

We attempted to determine whether the type of drug used (stimulant versus depressant) affected target selection decisions. The informants were asked to rate their drug state and to specify the type of drug being used at the time of the session and then to rate a number of potential burglary sites. The burglary attractiveness ratings obtained during these sessions demonstrated significant differences between burglars using cocaine and those using heroin and marijuana, and between those using drugs and those who were not under the influence. Cocaine users generally rated sites higher (more attractive) than did those who were not under the influence of drugs at the time of the staged activity and those who were using depressant drugs such as marijuana and heroin. Marijuana and heroin users rated sites less attractive as burglary sites than those

who were not using drugs at the time of the staged activity. The trend was toward more cautious decisions on the part of those using depressant drugs and toward more risky decisions when using cocaine, a stimulant. Both depressant and stimulant drug users were differentiated from those who were not using drugs at the time of the staged activity in the expected directions.

CO-OFFENDER EFFECTS
ON DECISION MAKING

One of the goals of the study was to determine whether the presence of co-offenders resulted in changes in decisions, particularly whether burglars took greater risks or were more conservative when working with partners. An increase toward the extreme (in either direction) of the individual responses following group discussion is called *group polarization* (Shaw, 1981).

As shown in Table 4.1, there was a trend toward more cautious decisions by groups compared to individual decisions of members of the groups. Informants tended to view potential targets as riskier after group discussion. This is consistent with our decision-making model discussed earlier. When selecting a target, the burglar must consider cues and cue clusters which he or she perceives to be proxies for occupancy, visibility, and accessibility. It is probable that more eyes perceive more risk cues, which would bias them toward caution. We noted this while monitoring group discussions. In groups, the informants often pointed out risk and occupancy cues that had been initially overlooked by their co-offenders during individual ratings.

During the interviews, however, informants generally reported greater willingness to take chances and to engage in risky behavior when working in groups. Almost all of the informants stated that they psyched each other up, explaining that they were braver when working as a part of a group than when alone. The following statements are representative:

I wouldn't do [burglarize] this house by myself. I'd get some other people to help me. I'd be too scared to do it alone.

Man, you gotta get a bunch of guys together and build up your nerve to do a house in this part of town.

You get a bunch of guys together and you psych each other up to do the job. If I got four or five people, I'd do any house out here.

The findings regarding group versus individual decisions appear to be contradictory. It is possible they are yet another example of the disparity between what the informants told us they did and what they actually did during field simulations of their past crimes. Although they expressed the belief that they were braver and took greater chances when working in a group, the staged activity analysis showed them to be more cautious. We suggest that both findings are valid. The informants did become braver and more "risky" when working in groups; however, this tendency toward risky behavior was

Table 4.1 Alone versus Group Attractiveness Ratings[1]

Site/time	HYPOTHETICAL CIRCUMSTANCES		
	At Present (Now)	Assuming No One Is Home	Assuming No One Is Home and $250 Cash Is Inside
BURGLAR RATINGS WHEN ALONE			
High risk/day	2.85 (60)	4.61 (51)	5.61 (43)
High risk/night	1.51 (59)	4.33 (55)	5.69 (55)
Previously hit/day	4.22 (59)	5.25 (48)	6.62 (42)
Previously hit/night	3.03 (58)	6.60 (53)	7.46 (52)
BURGLAR RATINGS WHEN IN A GROUP			
High risk/day	1.89 (61)	2.24 (49)	2.07 (28)
High risk/night	.41 (29)	3.55 (29)	4.20 (30)
Previously hit/day	2.75 (61)	3.44 (45)	3.33 (24)
Previously hit/night	1.88 (25)	5.43 (21)	6.59 (22)

[1]The individual burglary attractiveness ratings (means) of burglars alone and with co-offenders under the circumstances that actually prevailed at the time of the site inspection (now) and hypothetical circumstances for high-risk and previously hit sites as a function of day versus night staged analyses. The number of individual ratings of burglars alone and group ratings from those in groups from which each mean was obtained is given in parentheses. The attractiveness scale ranged 1–10, with higher numbers indicating the residence was more attractive.

offset by their increased capacity (when in groups) to perceive and respond to risk cues at the target site. The net effect was toward less risky acts.

Social Facilitation

In animal studies of social facilitation, researchers have found that the presence of co-actors of the same species increases activity of dominant or well-learned responses (Zajonc, 1965). In a classic study using human subjects, Floyd Allport (1920) concluded that the presence of co-actors increased output and performance on well-learned responses but that performance in situations requiring problem-solving or judgment skills was impaired. Zajonc (1965, 1980) has suggested that the presence of others, either as spectators or as co-actors, increases the individual's general arousal or drive level and may have the effect of either facilitating dominant well-learned responses (simple, well-learned responses) or inhibiting nondominant responses (complex, poorly learned responses). These studies suggest that burglars working in groups may tend to make errors in judgment and/or in technique, because of the increased level of arousal. These errors might contribute to a greater apprehension rate for burglars working in groups than for those working alone. The data support the hypothesis. All the informants reported a greater arousal level when working with a co-offender (psyching each other up), and their self-reported apprehension rate when working with partners was nearly five times greater than

when working alone, supporting the hypothesis that performance is impaired on complex, poorly learned responses.

Social facilitation studies also suggest that burglars working in groups could be expected to have a higher incidence of offending than when working alone. The data support this hypothesis as well. Several discussed hitting one house with one or more partners and then "going down the block," hitting several targets in a row.

Debbie confessed: "One night we hit this house here on the corner and then went down the block, hit 'em all. Once you get started, it's hard to stop." Several others discussed burglary sprees, hitting numerous targets in one night or during a single time period. No solo burglar in the sample mentioned multiple burglaries during a single time period.

SUMMARY

Our findings show that drug use and burglary are interrelated behaviors. Not only do burglars commit burglaries to obtain money to buy drugs, they also use drugs to initiate and facilitate the commission of their burglaries. Most of the informants in the study reported that drug use made them better burglars. To the extent that fear reduction, while under the moderate influence of alcohol or depressant drugs, facilitates parallel processing and allows burglars to be attentive to task-relevant cues in the environment, as well as aiding knowledge and skill recall, their self-reported improvement in performance appears to be accurate. This phenomenon may also be associated with enhancement of task ability attributable to state-dependent learning effects. The pleasure of searching for valuable items to steal, the intrinsic rewards from the proceeds of the burglary, the camaraderie of partying after the act, the reduction of fear through the use of drugs, and the failure of the criminal justice system to detect, apprehend, and punish burglars in any immediate and systematic way all serve to reinforce each step in the burglary process, increasing the likelihood that the behavior (burglary) will recur.

Heroin-using burglars tend to be more rational, more professional, and relatively less likely to be arrested than burglars using cocaine or speed. The heroin user was found to have some control over his or her drug intake and appeared to be capable of desisting from or reducing drug intake whenever necessary. This finding has implications for crime prevention, as it tends to show that heroin users are not completely controlled by their habit and do not require a fixed supply of drugs each and every day. Crime prevention strategies might therefore reduce criminal activity and not simply displace it to another form, time, or place.

Burglars using heroin and marijuana rated sites less attractive than burglars who were not using drugs at the time of the staged activity. Cocaine-using burglars rated sites more attractive than did burglars who were not under the influence of drugs at the time or those who were using marijuana or heroin. These findings suggest that drug type may affect decision making by increasing

or reducing central nervous system arousal, thereby increasing or decreasing the number of environmental cues utilized in the decision process.

Group effects (by increasing arousal) increase the level of risk the burglar finds acceptable in a burglary situation; however, the burglar perceives more risk cues when working in a group, and thus may not actually act in a more risky fashion. Increasing the level of acceptable risk while increasing attentiveness to environmental cues appears to have a moderate net effect of a shift toward caution. This increased caution, however, is not reflected in lower rates of apprehension. Burglars working in groups reported an apprehension rate at least five times greater than those working alone. Although many factors may account for this finding, we believe that impairment in performance on complex tasks, which has been noted with other behaviors in group situations, may also occur in group burglary. Furthermore, the increased incidence rates that we found in the group situation also increase the number of times the burglar is at risk and, thereby, the apprehension rate.

We were unable to determine the aggregate effect on decision making by burglars both working in groups and using drugs and/or alcohol—a state which is undoubtably common. Further research is recommended.

5

❖

Burglars and Fences

Our study of burglary led us to consider the important role of the fence—the market for the burglar's stolen goods. If burglary is the supply side of stolen property, then fencing is the demand side. Without a reliable outlet for stolen goods, burglary would have no point. Felson (1998, p. 38) states that the significance of the fence for producing more crime cannot be overstated. Without the opportunity to sell stolen goods, the thief is limited to stealing money only, or to very inefficient ways of selling on their own. We sought, therefore, to ascertain the dynamics of the thief–fence relationship; to determine the strategies employed by receivers of stolen property; and, how these strategies are implemented and understood by the participants in this activity.

The role of the fence in initiating and sustaining property crime has been recognized for centuries. F.L. Attenborough (1922), in *Laws of the Earliest English Kings*, refers to a law from 690 A.D., which prohibited "harboring stolen cattle." However, as Steffensmeier (1986) reports, until 1691, under common law, receiving stolen goods was only a misdemeanor. He stated, "While there was no strict law against receiving stolen property prior to the seventeenth century, it was recognized that the activity went on and that it was as bad as theft, which it may actually cause" (p. 63). Finally, in 1691 a statute (Act 3 and 4, William and Mary, c.9.s.4) made the fence an accessory after the fact and liable for severe corporal punishment or transportation. However, prosecution of the receiver was not possible unless the thief was first apprehended and convicted. In 1827, an act of Parliament made provision for an independent trial for the fence whether or not the thief was arrested (Act 7 and 8, Geo. IV c.29).

Perhaps the most notorious fence in criminal justice history was an Englishman, Jonathon Wild. McDonald (1980) described Wild as a notorious leader of a London criminal band of pickpockets, burglars, and other thieves. He set himself up as a "recoverer of stolen property," advertising in newspapers and pamphlets offering rewards for the return of stolen property with no questions asked. He bought the stolen goods and then conveyed them back to their original owners for a percent of their value. Thieves flocked to his "lost property office" with their stolen goods. Those items that were not claimed by their rightful owners, he altered so that they could not be identified and then sold them. Wild was so successful in this fencing venture that he even bought a ship to carry his plunder to Holland and other European ports. Thieves who did not cooperate with Wild were frequently turned in for the reward. It is estimated that he "captured" over 100 thieves during his fifteen-year career. In fact, as a well-known "thief taker" he was consulted by the Privy Council on occasion for his advice on crime control. However, becoming a public figure is something that no criminal should aspire to, for his high profile eventually brought him down. A notorious criminal who had been captured by Wild escaped from prison and publicly testified to Wild's activities. Soon other witnesses began to appear and Wild's activities resulted in his arrest and conviction. He was hanged in 1725 (McDonald, 1980).

STATE OF KNOWLEDGE ABOUT FENCES AND FENCING

Despite the fence's acknowledged contribution to crime, there has been a paucity of systematic study of this important category of offender. Due to the clandestine nature of the fence's activities, it is not surprising that so little research has been done. The professional fence has attracted the attention of some researchers, policy makers, and law enforcers (Blakey and Goldsmith, 1976; Klockars, 1974; Senate Select Committee, 1973; Steffensmeier, 1986; Walsh, 1977; Maguire, 1982). Taken as a whole, although these studies provide a good overview of the activities of the professional fence, they ignore almost completely other categories of receivers. However, the nonprofessional receiver has not been overlooked completely. Hall (1952) included part-time receivers in his typology of fences. He identified the "lay receiver," who buys for personal consumption, and the "occasional receiver," who purchases for resale, but only infrequently. Stuart Henry (1978), who studied property crimes committed by ordinary people in legitimate jobs, concluded that receiving stolen property is not exclusively the province of professional criminals, but is an "everyday feature of ordinary people's lives." He states:

> The artificial distinction between "honest" and "dishonest" masks the fact that the hidden economy is the on-the-side, illegal activity of "honest" people who have legitimate jobs and who would never admit to being dishonest. (p. 12)

Henry found that many, otherwise legitimate businessmen purchased stolen property when such purchases could be passed on to their customers at a profit.

Cromwell and McElrath (1994) surveyed 739 randomly selected adults in a southwestern city. Respondents were asked if they had ever been offered stolen property for sale, if they had bought stolen property, and if they had friends or neighbors who had bought stolen goods. Thirty-six percent reported having been offered stolen goods. Thirteen percent had knowingly bought stolen goods and 39 percent reported that friends had bought stolen items. They reported that opportunity to purchase stolen goods and the motivation to buy them is related to a person's age, gender, ethnicity, and income. They stated:

> Routine activities theory predicts that buyers and sellers of stolen property must converge in time and space before an illegal transaction can occur. This convergence is facilitated when the lifestyles of buyers and sellers bring them together . . . Younger persons and males were much more likely than older persons and females to be offered stolen goods for use in their home. These groups are also more likely to engage in "high risk" activities which might bring them into physical proximity with sellers of stolen goods. (p. 306)

A recent British study, The British Crime Survey (BCS), revealed that a large number of persons are offered stolen property by thieves. Eleven percent of respondents said that they had been offered stolen property in the previous year. A further 11 percent admitted that they had bought stolen goods in the past five years, while 70 percent thought that at least some of their friends and neighbors had purchased stolen goods for use in their home (Sutton, 1998). Further, the Youth Lifestyle Survey, also conducted in England, found that 49 percent of youths aged fourteen to twenty five years, who admitted offending in the last year, admitted that they had bought or sold stolen property in that period (Graham and Bowling, 1995).

There is little reliable and valid information regarding the extent of the fencing activities among nonprofessional receivers of stolen property, or the degree to which these amateur fences contribute to the initiation and continuing support of property crime. Some earlier studies concluded that thieves are unable to deal directly with the consuming public and must therefore operate through middlemen who have the financial resources to purchase stolen goods and the contacts to help in their redistribution (Blakey and Goldsmith, p. 1515). Indeed, this is true in large-scale theft where a thief must dispose of a truckload of television sets or a collection of fine jewelry. Most property crime, however, involves smaller quantities of stolen goods, of lesser value. Televisions, computers, CD players, car radios, most jewelry, handguns, VCRs, microwave ovens—the items that constitute the loot of the average burglar or shoplifter—may be redistributed without the assistance of a professional fence. The thief may sell many of these items directly to the ultimate consumer, to individuals who know or suspect that the items they buy are stolen property.

Some items may be traded for drugs, or sold to part-time receivers—those whose primary business activity is something other than buying and selling stolen property. Other stolen merchandise may be sold in pawn shops, flea markets, and garage sales to consumers who do not know or suspect that it was stolen.

We found that many burglars sought alternative outlets for their stolen goods. They reported selling their stolen items to ordinary citizens in bars, stores, parking lots, and even door-to-door. Others had regular customers for certain types of goods, and still others sold to otherwise legitimate businesses (bars, truck stops, etc.) who were known to be open to an opportunity to buy stolen items.

In order to understand how burglars and other thieves converted stolen property to cash, we interviewed both thieves and those who bought from them. We analyzed the thief's perspective by observations and interviews with active burglars and shoplifters, and through analysis of statements given to the police by arrested burglars and shoplifters. We obtained the receiver's outlook through interviews with professional and nonprofessional fences. We believe that amateur receivers who purchase stolen property do so primarily for personal consumption.

Interviews with Burglars

Burglar subjects were asked to describe (1) the process of locating and selecting a buyer for property they stole; (2) how items obtained in burglaries are sold or bartered; (3) the extent to which the fence determines the goods to be stolen; (4) the extent to which receivers provide aid and strategy to thieves in selecting targets; (5) the decision-making processes that determine what items are offered to which receivers; (6) the prices expected and paid for certain items; and (7) the extent, if any, to which fences specialize in one type or class of merchandise.

Interviews with Fences and Other Receivers

During the course of this study our burglar informants introduced us to many of their regular receivers. Because we had been vouched for by burglars whom they knew and trusted, we had little trouble in obtaining their consent to be interviewed. We approached eight fences in this manner and six of them agreed to be interviewed. Four of them were interviewed extensively over several days or weeks. Interviews with two others were concluded in a session lasting an hour or two. One, a professional fence, allowed us to observe his activities from the back room of a small liquor store, which was a front for his fencing activities.

We also interviewed nineteen persons who had purchased stolen property directly from a thief. These subjects were students in our classes, friends and acquaintances, or friends of friends who heard about the study and agreed to talk to us about their experiences. Some of these individuals were one-time purchasers only. Others, however, were regular customers of a thief or thieves.

These interviews—with thieves, fences, and others who knowingly bought stolen property—were subjected to qualitative analysis wherein we derived patterns and constructed typologies from the extensive descriptions.

Interviews with Professional Burglars and Fences

Professional burglars must have reliable outlets for their stolen merchandise. Most sell their goods to one or more professional fences. Dealing directly with the consumer is too irregular and an uncertain way of doing business. Other burglars, however, have limited access to the professional fence. Novice burglars, juveniles, and drug addicts often find it hard to establish regular business relationships with fences. Novices and juvenile burglars do not often steal "quality" merchandise and have not been "tested" regarding their trustworthiness. Drug addicts have a similar handicap in marketing their goods. They are considered unreliable and untrustworthy because of their drug habits. While several addict-burglars reported that they occasionally sold their stolen merchandise to a professional fence, most had to seek less rewarding and more risky alternative channels for their goods. Many resorted regularly to direct sales to the consuming public. One young burglar, who regularly sold his stolen goods directly to consumers, said: "I hear about somebody who want a TV or a VCR. I ask 'em how much they want to pay, and then I go get them one. If I already got some stuff, I ask around if anybody want to buy it."

A heroin-addict-burglar reported: "I sell my stuff to [a local fence, name deleted] when I can. Sometimes he buys stuff from me. Most of the time he don't. He don't trust addicts."

Another informant told the interviewer that he had regular customers for his merchandise. He described his "self-fencing" in the following manner:

> There is this lady who buys big dresses—like bigger than size sixteen. She pays good too. Another lady will buy jewelry and stuff if I have it. I know about ten people who buy meat. Whatever is on the price tag, they give me half price. There is even a policeman—he used to be a policeman—he buys guns if I get one.

Most of the burglars interviewed would have preferred to sell their goods to a fence. They believed the fence to be a more reliable and less risky market. However, of the thirty informants in the study, only seven (23 percent) reported that they could absolutely depend on the professional fences in the community to take their goods. Others reported only occasional business dealings with professional fences. The following statement was typical: "If I get guns, Not junk—like Saturday-nite specials—stuff like Smith and Wessons—I can sell to the fences. I sold some big diamond rings and a Rolex to [local fence, name deleted] last year. They don't buy TVs and VCRs though."

Professional fences reported a strong aversion to doing business with drug addicts and juveniles. However, one fence, while expressing his contempt for drug addicts, bought stolen items from several obvious drug users while we were observing. He explained that, "So many thieves these days are addicts

that you got to do a little business with them or you go broke." Another fence, more adamant in his refusal to do business with drug addicts, posted a sign over his cash register. It stated, "NO ADDICTS."

The fences reported that amateurs, drug users, "kids," and other "flakes," could not be trusted. They "snitch" and turn in their buyers when arrested. Professional thieves do not so readily "give up" their meal tickets—their market for stolen goods. Several reported that they would give up their co-offenders before their fence. One expressed his attitude as follows: "Shit! Thieves are easy to find. I can get somebody to help me do a crime anywhere. Fences—they harder to replace. You turn in [local fences] and nobody gonna do no business with you after that."

Interviews with Nonprofessional Receivers

We also interviewed nineteen nonprofessional receivers. These were persons who had bought stolen items for personal consumption and/or resale, but who did not depend upon fencing for all or most of their livelihood. Some had bought stolen property only once or twice. Others were regular consumers of stolen goods. One of these fence/consumers, a college professor who had been buying clothing for himself and his family from a group of burglars and shoplifters for over twenty years, described his activities as follows: "I go to [department store] and pick out what I want, and tell [thief]. He brings it around in a few days. I pay one-third of the price tag."

A college student reported: "I know this guy. He's a pot head. He gets speakers and CD players, and all kind of stuff like that. I've bought stuff from him a lot."

A homemaker in a low-income neighborhood explained how she became a customer of a shoplifter: "My friend said she bought meat from this drug addict. She said she could get me some meat at half price. First, I bought some steaks for half price. Now he comes by my house every payday and we get all our meat from him. Other stuff too, sometimes."

More than one-half (n = 11) of the nonprofessional receivers we interviewed own or are employed by legitimate businesses, and occasionally buy stolen property at their place of business, primarily for resale. But, unlike the professional fence, they do not rely on buying and selling stolen property as their principal means of livelihood. To them, fencing is a part-time enterprise, secondary to, but usually associated with, their primary business activity. One of these part-time receivers justified his regular purchases from a thief, saying: "It's not like you have anything to do with the guy stealing the stuff. He has already stole it. If I didn't buy it someone else would. I just take advantage of a good deal when I can. It's good business."

Another explained, saying: "I don't even know for sure the stuff is hot. All I know is I can buy brand new tires for twenty bucks apiece. The last ones I got from him were Michelins . . . I'm going to turn that down?"

A dry-cleaner whose sideline was buying and selling stolen men's suits from shoplifters reported: "I can put them in a bag and run them in with my

regular cleaning. I don't make a big profit. Some weeks I don't buy anything. Mostly I sell to some friends and family. It helps out when business is slow."

Analysis of Arrest Reports

We analyzed 190 statements (confessions) given to police by arrested burglars in the study jurisdiction for one year, in which the burglars told police where and how they had disposed of the stolen property. The alleged receiver(s) of the stolen property were noted and classified as either a professional fence, drug-dealer, part-time receiver, ordinary citizen, etc., through information derived as follows: that contained in the police report; with the help of knowledgeable police detectives; with the assistance of thief "informants"; or, in some cases, through our own knowledge of the criminal community. Other information in the police report which related to the receiver (the thief's reason for choosing a particular receiver or class of receiver, the amount paid for the items, etc.) was also analyzed. The analysis revealed that only 21 percent of the stolen property was sold to professional fences. More than half (56.4 percent) was sold to nonprofessional receivers, including drug dealers. Only 12.1 percent was sold to pawn shops. The remaining 10.5 percent was reported to have been kept by the thief for personal consumption, thrown away, given away, or recovered by police before redistribution. The following statements are representative:

We took the microwave to [address deleted] and we sold it to an elderly Mexican lady for $30.

I traded this stuff [cartons of cigarettes] to a man named Mario on the south side for heroin.

The place where we took the guns was a house on [street name deleted] in [town]. A man named [name deleted] lives there. He is in a motorcycle gang named the Outlaws. They buy guns.

Then I went back to the 7-11 and sold the VCR to [a customer in the parking lot]. I sold the disc player and the VCR to [name deleted] at [name deleted] Liquor Store.

I went in [local tavern] and asked if anyone wanted to buy some cigarettes. Three or four people asked me how much. All I had was Salems and they wanted Marlboros. The bartender said he'd take 'em and sell them to some guy he knows smokes Salems.

I sold the disc player and the VCR to [name deleted] at [name deleted] liquor store.

About two weeks ago I met a man named [name deleted]. I met him through the wife of a friend of mine. She told me that [name deleted] might be willing to buy some stolen TV's I had from a burglary a few days before. I took the TV's over there and we plugged them in to see if they worked, and they did and he gave me $50 each for them.

WHY BUY STOLEN PROPERTY?

Buying stolen property involves many different motives. It represents a means of livelihood for some people—individuals who earn all or a significant proportion of their income from fencing. For others, as Steffensmeier (1986) suggests, "fencing they do more or less helps keep them afloat, get over the hump in their legitimate business, or gives them a little extra pocket money" (p. 118). For many others, buying (and occasionally selling) stolen property is a means of economic adaptation. Henry (1978) and Smith (1987) refer to this activity as constituting an "informal economy" or "hidden economy." Participation means more than stretching the dollar. It may, as Gaughan and Ferman (1987) suggest, be a means of economic survival. They write:

A number of case studies have shown that low income communities rely on informal economic resources. The importance of hustling in the black ghetto, the persistence of tight kinship networks in working-class urban communities, and the increasing visibility of street peddlers and entertainers testify to this. (p. 23)

Several informants told us that they could not survive [economically] without "hustling." One reported: "I buy my baby's clothes from this booster [shoplifter]. He sells lots of stuff—even deodorant, aspirin, and medicine. I get cigarettes from another thief. My mother gets all her meat from a booster."

A housewife/informant reported that she occasionally bought from a burglar of her acquaintance and then resold some of the various items. She stated that the income from this source allowed her to stay at home with her children rather than having to seek outside employment.

While for some, buying and/or selling stolen property was purely economic activity, we were unable to differentiate subjective motivations from economic motivations in many transactions. Psychosocial dynamics were often inextricably bound with economic motives. Some informants reported that they simply could not resist a bargain. Both thieves and receivers reported that "getting a good deal" was an important motivation for the buyer of stolen goods. Some reported buying items for which they had no immediate use, because the "price was right" or that they liked "beating the system." For still others, the occasional purchase of stolen property provided excitement in an otherwise pedestrian existence. One lawyer, for instance, asserted that he bought stolen property not just because he wanted certain items or for the money he might make reselling the items, but also for the "insider feeling" he got through these associations (also see Shover, 1971, p. 153). Another "amateur" receiver reported that she was a member of a group of office workers who bought clothing from several shoplifters who "made the rounds" in various offices and businesses in the area. The women frequently placed orders for items of clothing and paid a prearranged price for the items when the shoplifter returned with the goods. Our informant revealed that the items they purchased were often bought as gifts for friends and relatives. She described a sort of "party atmosphere" around the office on the day the

shoplifter was due to arrive with the goods they had ordered days before. As described by our informant, the transaction appeared to be as much social as economic in nature.

One theme that appeared to characterize nonprofessional receivers was the tendency to neutralize or rationalize their involvement in the purchase of stolen property. Almost all of those interviewed disassociated themselves from the theft, and by extension, the victim(s). Many rationalized that "It was already stolen. If I didn't buy it, someone would." They appeared to view the purchase of stolen property as victimless crime, if crime at all. Many neutralized their purchases as "Simply getting a bargain," or that the victim was an insurance company or a big business that "expects to lose a certain amount of merchandise," and makes up for the loss by increasing prices. Many reported that they did not know for sure that the items were stolen. One informant justified her purchase of a new VCR for $50, stating: "Okay, it's maybe too good a deal to be completely honest. I asked him if it was stolen and he said, 'No,' and I took his word for it. That's all I can do. I don't want to know either."

Burglars and other thieves appeared to intuitively understand the psychology of selling stolen property directly to the consumer. Most reported that the items must not be explicitly represented as stolen, yet the buyer must believe them to be illegally obtained, and therefore a "good deal." One burglar/informant occasionally purchased cheap costume jewelry from a discount store and sold it as genuine on street corners to passersby. While he did not specifically represent the jewelry as stolen, he implied that it was. He reported that he usually made a good profit from this scam. He concluded: "People are basically dishonest. They just don't like to admit it to themselves."

Shover's (1971) informant described the same phenomenon, stating: "It's the excitement of buying a piece of stolen goods. If you told them . . . that it was legitimate, they wouldn't buy it" (p. 153).

Several burglars reported that they devised elaborate stories about the source of their stolen items. They explained that buyers like a good story, even if they don't really believe it. The cover story serves to relieve the buyer's anxiety over buying stolen property. An articulate burglar, a college graduate who turned to burglary after becoming addicted to heroin, analyzed the citizen-receivers he did business with, saying:

People need to feel good about themselves. Most folks can't accept that they are as crooked as us [burglars]. You gotta help 'em out a little. Give 'em a story about the stuff. They know you're lying. Doesn't matter. They need it to keep you and them separated in their minds. You're the thief and they're the good guys.

A TYPOLOGY OF RECEIVERS

It is impossible to characterize those who buy stolen property as a homogeneous category. Rather, they are a diverse group ranging from professional criminals with ties to organized crime (Klockars, 1974; Steffensmeier, 1986) to respected citizens such as schoolteachers, business-persons and office workers

who buy stolen goods for personal consumption (Henry; Cromwell and McElrath). They may be differentiated by: (1) the frequency with which they purchase stolen property; (2) the scale or volume of purchases of stolen property; (3) the purpose of purchase (for personal consumption or for resale); and (4) the level of commitment to purchasing stolen property. On the basis of these criteria, we distinguished six categories of receivers or fences:

1. Professional fences
2. Part-time fences
3. Professionals who trade their services for stolen property
4. Neighborhood hustlers
5. Drug dealers who barter drugs for stolen property
6. Amateurs

Professional Fences

The professional fence is one whose principal enterprise is the purchase and redistribution of stolen property (Blakey & Goldsmith, 1976; Chappell & Walsh, 1974; Klockars; Steffensmeier, 1986). Professional receivers may transact for any stolen property for which there is a resale potential, or may specialize in stolen property that they can commingle with their legitimate stock or legitimate business (e.g., jewelry, dry cleaning, appliance sales or service). The professional receiver generally makes purchases directly from the thief and almost exclusively for resale. These receivers operate proactively, establishing a reliable and persistent flow of merchandise and buying regularly and on a large scale. As a result of this commitment, the professional receiver acquires "a reputation among law breakers, law enforcers and others in the criminal community" (Klockars, p. 172). Although professional fences frequently operate "legitimate from a burglar of her acquaintance" businesses as fronts for their fencing activities, fencing is their primary occupation.

Part-time Fences

The part-time fence functions in a somewhat nebulous domain between the true professional fence and other categories of receivers. The part-time fence is differentiated from the "professional" fence by frequency of purchase, volume of business, and degree of commitment to the fencing enterprise. Usually they do not buy as regularly as do professional fences, nor do they buy in volume. Further, part-time fences do not depend on fencing as their principal means of livelihood. We identified two general sub-types of part-time fences: (a) the passive receiver—who purchases stolen goods either for personal use, or for resale to an undifferentiated secondary consumer; and (b) the proactive receiver—who buys for resale only, and who may take an active role in the theft by placing orders for specific merchandise and providing offenders with information about potentially lucrative targets for burglary in the same way as professional fences.

Passive buyers are known (by thieves) to be buyers of stolen goods. They are "passive" because they do not actively solicit thieves as suppliers, nor do they contract to buy certain items from thieves. Their commitment as receivers is only at the level of being occasionally available to buy certain items of stolen property when offered by a thief. We identified several passive buyers during the study, including a truck stop operator who bought stolen tires and tools, the manager of a video rental business who bought stolen VCRs and video-tapes, and a jewelry store proprietor who bought gold jewelry and silverware. Like all part-time receivers, the passive receiver does not buy in volume, and does not depend on fencing as a principal means of livelihood. They may inte-grate the stolen items into their regular stock, or may personally use the stolen goods—as with the case of an automobile mechanic who buys stolen tools. Like all part-time fences, they are not considered reliable outlets by thieves. They buy only when they have funds available, and/or when they need the particular item(s) offered by the thief. They usually do not have in mind a specific customer to whom they might resell the merchandise.

Proactive receivers mimic professional fences in many respects; however, they do not rely on buying and selling stolen goods for the major part of their livelihood. Their fencing activity is an on-the-side activity, part-time crime. The proactive buyer may contract with a thief for certain items for which he or she has a market. They may actually "take orders" from customers for certain items and arrange to purchase those items from a thief or thieves. Several burglar/shoplifter informants reported that they occasionally stole certain items "on order" from both professional fences and from part-time receivers.

The part-time receiver might even have greater access than the profes-sional fence to strategic information regarding potential victims. Because they are otherwise legitimate citizens and businesspersons, they may be trusted by their colleagues and friends with information regarding their possessions, schedules, and security precautions.

We identified three proactive part-time fences. They were each otherwise legitimate businesspersons. One owned a jewelry store and the majority of his income was from the legitimate profits of the store. However, he occasionally contracted to buy certain specific items of jewelry from a professional thief. In many cases the jeweler had originally sold the items to the victim—only to steal them back. Another proactive part-time receiver, a gunsmith, gained extensive knowledge about a customer's gun collection through his profession, and used that information to provide inside information to a thief about security arrange-ments and particular items to be stolen. In another case, a pawnbroker provided a thief with descriptions of a customer's jewelry and the details of the customer's vacation plans, which the customer had revealed to him during a conversation.

Professionals Who Trade Services for Stolen Property

These fences are persons whose legitimate occupations place them in close association and interaction with thieves, as in the case of police officers, crimi-nal defense attorneys, or bail bond agents. These receivers may operate from

a different economic motivation than other receivers in that they stand to lose financially by refusing to participate in the redistribution of stolen property. This is particularly true for bail bond agents and criminal defense attorneys, who may provide legitimate professional services to property offenders who cannot pay for these services with anything but stolen property (or the proceeds from their illegal activities). Thieves constitute a significant market for the services that these receivers provide legitimately. To refuse such trade would eliminate these "customers" and would severely curtail earnings. For some, it is but a small step from accepting stolen property in return for professional services, to placing orders for items to be stolen. During the study, a bail bond agent showed the interviewer a matched pair of stainless steel .357 magnum revolvers that had been stolen for him "on order" by a client for whom he had posted bond. He freely acknowledged accepting stolen property occasionally in exchange for his services, justifying his actions by saying, "When they are in a bind and don't have any money, I try to help out." Another individual, a criminal defense lawyer, was completely candid about his occasional purchases of stolen property from clients, enthusiastically describing items he had received in exchange for his legal services. He described how he had agreed to represent a burglar in a criminal case, telling him that he wanted a gold Rolex in exchange for his services. He proudly displayed the $12,000 watch to the interviewer and stated, "This is a special order."

Neighborhood Hustlers

The neighborhood hustler buys and sells stolen property as one of many hustles—small-time crime and confidence games—which provide a [usually] marginal living outside the conventional economic system. The neighborhood hustler may be a small-time fence, or he or she may be a middleman who brings thieves and customers together, earning a percentage of the sale for service rendered. The neighborhood hustler may also be a burglar who, on occasion, tries a hand at marketing stolen items for others. By definition, he or she is a small-time operator (Blakey and Goldsmith). Most do not have a place of business, as such. Instead, they work out of the trunk of a car, or from their home. One such entrepreneur described himself as follows: "I'm a hustler. I can get you what you want. You got something you want to sell? Tell me. I know where to go and who to see. Ain't nothing happens over here in the Flats [the area of town where he lived] that I don't know about." According to others who knew him, although he was grossly exaggerating his abilities, he was an almost stereotypical neighborhood hustler. Few experienced thieves would trust him to buy directly or to sell their merchandise for them. Several informants described him as a snitch whose hustles included "giving up" the thieves with whom he did business. He was therefore limited to buying from juveniles, drug addicts, and novice thieves who could not market their goods in a more reliable manner.

For some, hustling involves both buying stolen goods for personal consumption, and dealing in stolen merchandise. One such neighborhood hustler

among our informants bought cigarettes, food, and clothing for personal use, and bought other items for resale. At the time of our interview, she had recently bought twenty rolls of roofing tar paper and 100 gallons of house paint from a thief and resold the items to a building contractor for a $75 profit. Her hustles also included some low-level street drug dealing, which occasionally involved bartering drugs for stolen goods, which she then resold.

Drug Dealers Who Barter Drugs for Stolen Property

Although not every drug dealer will barter for drugs, our interviews with thieves and fences suggest that many street level dealers consider fencing and drug sales to be logically compatible enterprises. There are two apparent economic motivations for their willingness to barter: (1) bartering increases their drug sales, opening their market to those with stolen property but without cash; and (2) they can increase their profits by marketing the stolen property at a price well above that given in trade to the addict/thief. One such fence, in discussing the advantages of the arrangement, said: "Lot of people come to me 'cause I'll take trades. Won't take no junk or TVs or shit like that. If they got guns, jewelry—then we can do business."

Several of the burglar/drug users we interviewed regularly bartered stolen property for drugs. Rather than searching for an outlet for the goods, they went directly to the drug dealer and obtained drugs in exchange. Although they reported that they did not receive the best possible price for their merchandise from the drug dealer, the speed and efficiency of the operation made the arrangement attractive. One subject said, "This is like one-stop shopping." Wright and Decker also found that some burglars in their study sold their stolen goods to drug dealers or traded them for drugs.

> Many of the tough inner-city neighborhoods of St. Louis have an informal economy that operates in part on the sale of stolen property. Local drug dealers often play a prominent role in this economy, both as buyers and sellers, because they have access to ready cash and good illicit connections to potential customers. (p. 181)

One of their informants explained:"Most of the time I want to buy drugs, so I take them stuff to the drug man. Instead of giving me money—he don't want to give out money 'cause he's making money—so he'll trade you his merchandise for your merchandise" (p. 182).

Amateurs

With the exception of the professional thieves in the sample (n = 5) all had sold their goods directly to consumers on one or more occasions. The least experienced, the juvenile and drug-using thieves, were most likely to sell directly to the consumer on a regular basis. We distinguished two general categories of amateur receivers: (1) strangers approached in public places; and (2) persons with whom the thief has developed a relationship and who buys more or less regularly, for personal consumption.

Approaching strangers in public places is risky behavior with a relatively low success rate. It is looked upon with contempt by almost all thieves, and practiced regularly only by those with no other outlets available for their merchandise. Juveniles and drug addicts are most likely to use this technique for disposing of their merchandise. While many thieves in our study expressed their disdain for selling stolen items in this manner, the analysis of confessions given to police by burglars and other thieves revealed that much of the stolen items of these thieves was sold in this manner. Furthermore, many of the nonprofessional receivers we interviewed reported that they had previously bought stolen items from thieves who approached them in a public place. This suggests that the practice may be more widespread than was indicated in the interviews with burglars.

Wright and Decker also found that a percentage of their burglar subjects approached strangers in public places offering their stolen goods for sale. Twelve of ninety offenders in their sample said they usually sold, at least in part, to strangers. One of their subjects reported: "Man, just like if I see you on the street I walk up and say, 'Hey, you want to buy a brand new nineteen-inch color TV?' You say, 'Yeah,' and give me $75. I'll plug it up for you" (p. 189).

Our burglar informants expressed similar sentiments:

I hang at the parking lot at [local chain food store] when I got something to sell. I go up to people that looks like they might buy something. Ask them if they wanna buy whatever I got.

Don't go up to no rich looking people or old people. Mostly young white dudes is interested.

Course, ya gotta be careful cause cops is mostly like that too—young, white dudes.

A second category of amateur receivers includes those who have developed relationships with one or more thieves and buy stolen property with some regularity. Most buy primarily for personal consumption. Others occasionally resell the stolen property they buy. Several reported reselling their "hot" merchandise at garage sales or through flea markets. Two of the "amateurs" resold the merchandise to friends and coworkers. One amateur fence, a public schoolteacher, began her criminal career when she was approached by a student who offered her a "really good deal" on a microwave oven. She stated that she originally bought the oven to help the student, whose family was suffering financial problems. Afterward, the student began to offer her "bargains" regularly, and she became a frequent customer. Eventually she began to offer her colleagues the opportunity to "get in on a good deal," and even posted the following note in the teachers' lounge:

> NEED ATV, VCR, MICROWAVE, ETC.?????
> SEE ME BEFORE YOU BUY.
> ½ OFF RETAIL.

Usually the teacher did not profit financially in this exchange. Instead, she garnered the goodwill and appreciation of those to whom she afforded merchandise at well below wholesale prices. Although she admitted to the interviewer that she "probably knew, deep down inside" that the items were stolen, she had never previously admitted it to herself. In explaining her motivation for purchasing goods in such an unconventional manner, she ironically described them as "a real steal."

Some individuals begin as amateur fences and become more deeply involved as a result of the irresistible gains and the virtual absence of sanctions entailed in purchasing stolen property. The overwhelming increase in profits and the thrill of "beating the system" (or at least making a good deal) tempt them into increasing their participation in the distribution of stolen property. One such amateur, turned part-time fence—a social worker—began her fencing activities when her husband purchased a household appliance from a thief he met in the course of his business as a plumber. At first their purchases were for their own consumption. Later, they bought Christmas presents for family members. Eventually they established a thriving family business buying stolen property from thieves and selling it in garage sales and flea markets, as well as to amateur receivers cultivated by the husband through his business colleagues and customers. The informant told the interviewer that she and her husband had put their son through college with the proceeds.

SUMMARY

The extent to which fences contribute to the incidence of property theft has been a central issue of debate. In the late 18th century, English magistrate Patrick Colquhoun (1797) called for vigorous action against fences in London, stating, "Nothing can be more just than the old observation, 'that if there were no Receivers there would be no Thieves'" (p. 298). Colquhoun's observation continues to have currency. Many believe that if fences could be put out of business, property crime rates would be dramatically reduced (Blakey and Goldsmith; Walsh, 1977). The fence is portrayed as not only providing a market for stolen goods, but also serving as an instigator and initiator of property theft.

This perspective has been criticized by other observers who argue that the "conception of the fence's role in property theft is bigger and more important than it ought to be, and that the involvement of other participants in an illegal trade is overlooked" (Steffensmeier, 1986, p. 285). Stuart Henry argues that viewing the fence as the prime mover of property theft rests on pretending that real crimes are committed by "real" criminals, not by ordinary people, and certainly not by oneself (cited in Steffensmeier, 1986, p. 286).

The extent to which ordinary people participate in the hidden economy (buying and selling stolen goods) is yet undetermined. However, our findings suggest that this part-time crime is ubiquitous (see also Henry; Cromwell and

McElrath; Sutton, 1998). Unlike the professional fence, these individuals do not perceive themselves as criminal, or as part of the impetus for property crime. Yet, they provide a ready market for stolen property, particularly for the young, inexperienced, and drug-addicted thieves who lack connections with professional fences.

Markets for stolen goods provide the catalyst and continuing motivation for property. Some young burglars find that they cannot sell their stolen goods successfully and consequently soon give up stealing. However, burglars who are able to convert their goods to cash at the first attempt may continue to repeat this rewarding behavior. Mitigating the market for stolen goods might have a positive effect on halting some criminal careers before they begin (Sutton et al., 2001).

These relatively unstudied channels of redistribution of stolen property may have important implications for crime control. Research that identifies these channels and determines the extent to which stolen property is purchased directly by the consuming public or by "otherwise honest" businesspeople and citizens will assist in the development of strategies to inhibit and disrupt the distribution process.

6

❖

Desisting from Burglary

Shover (1996, p. 119) states that one of the most striking characteristics of those who commit property crimes is their youth. It is well established that the ages fifteen to twenty-four years represent the "at risk" years for crime. Persons age twenty to twenty-five years account for only 21 percent of the population in the United States, but almost 55 percent of all arrests (U.S. Census Bureau, 1998; Federal Bureau of Investigation, 1999). Crime peaks between the ages of seventeen to eighteen years and then declines rapidly. Most desist from crime within months or, at most, a few years after committing their first offense. A small percentage, however, persist. Wolfgang and his associates (1972) followed over 9,000 males born in Philadelphia in 1945. They found that about 6 percent of those committed more than one-half of all serious crimes committed by the group by age eighteen years (Wolfgang, Figlio, and Sellin, 1972). These chronic offenders continued their criminal careers well into adulthood. Even these, however, tend to reduce or desist from their criminal activity as they grow older.

Desistance has been a controversial topic in criminology. Research has generally shown a decline in criminal activity as the individual ages (Cohen and Land, 1987; Glassner, Ksander, Berg, and Johnson, 1983; Hirschi and Gottfredson, 1983; Wilson and Herrnstein, 1985; Wolfgang, Figlio, and Sellin). Some criminologists conclude that age is a constant and that crime rates decline steadily after peaking in the early adult years. Hirschi and Gottfredson (1983), the champions of this position, argue that age does not interact with other variables and has a direct effect on crime rates. It is a variable

independent of other variables. This age–crime curve is consistent over time, space, and culture.

Others suggest that there are social factors associated with age such as employment, education, lifestyle, peer relations, social control, and marriage that explain the "aging-out" phenomenon. From this perspective, Siegel (1989) asserts, "Crime would then be conceived of as a type of social event that takes on different meanings at different times in a person's life" (p. 73).

Farrington (1986) and Blumstein and his associates (Blumstein, Cohen, and Farrington, 1988) maintain that persons begin to specialize in certain criminal activities as they age and neither the frequency nor the type of an individual's criminal activity is constant. This position advocates studying criminality as a career, undergoing evolving patterns or cycles in a person's lifetime. For instance, Steffensmeier and his associates (Steffensmeier, Allen, Harer, and Streifel, 1987) found that although the rates for some crimes decline with age, others such as fraud, embezzlement, and gambling are less likely to decline with maturity.

Other age–related factors are associated with criminality. Greenburg (1985) and Farrington have shown that a person who begins criminal patterns at an early age and who gains an official record is more likely to continue in criminal activity.

Despite the controversy over how age is related to crime, there is little doubt that crime rates decline with age. There are a number of explanations for the aging-out phenomenon. Trasler (1987) suggests that crime by youths is exciting and fun, and provides social activity in an otherwise boring and unsympathetic world. As they grow older their life patterns are inconsistent with crime—they literally grow out of crime.

Wilson and Herrnstein present an explanation that is closely linked to socialization. Adolescent deviance is associated with the need for conventionally unattainable money and sex and reinforced by peers who defy conventional morality. Their energy and strength, combined with a lack of economic skills and with relationships with peers, create the conditions favorable to crime. As the individual matures, the small gains from petty crimes lose their attractiveness and legitimate sources of money, sex, alcohol, and status become available. In addition, adulthood brings powerful ties to conventional society, including jobs and the acquisition of a family. Adult peers usually espouse values that are in opposition to risk-taking and law violation.

Charles Tittle (1988) maintains that aging-out-of-crime is more a matter of interpersonal relationships than of any emotional or physical processes. He suggests that children who get into trouble early in life and are labeled by authorities as troublemakers may have little choice but to pursue a criminal career. Even these individuals will eventually slow down. Crime is too physically demanding, too dangerous, and emotionally taxing—and the punishments too harsh and long-lasting—to be a way of life for most people.

Another view considers desistance to be associated with the fear of punishment. Glassner et al. (1983) associates aging-out-of-crime with the knowledge by youth that once they have reached the age when they become

subject to the jurisdiction of adult courts and penal institutions, punishment will be decidedly harsher.

Shover (1985, 1996, p. 124) presents a *career contingencies* approach to understanding desistance. He states that changes in offenders' objective circumstances have the effect of maintaining them in their criminal career path, changing their criminal behavior, or causing them to desist. Some conditions cause a turning away from crime and others have an opposite effect. Those conditions that tend to contribute to desistance are those which strengthen conventional social bonds, activities, and rewards. Economic self-sufficiency (obtaining and holding a job), positive interpersonal relationships with non-criminal others, and integration into "law abiding communities" (including marriage and family) have an indisputable role in turning away from criminal disputes (Shover, 1996, pp. 124–7).

Shover (1996) also argues that one of the primary dynamics behind desistance is fear of increasingly severe penalties and the concomitant fear of losing valuable time to imprisonment. As one of his subjects stated while interviewed in prison:

> *"I'm older [now] and don't have much time. I guess you start looking at how much time you have left, and what to do with that time. . .I'm forty-two now. I got twenty years left, and I'm sitting here doing this dead time, you know, nothing out of my life but dead time. . . . Every year that goes by, it seems like it's quicker, you know. Life, before you're twenty-one it seems like it's forever, before you turn twenty-one. And after you do, time seems like it's flying by." (p. 133)*

Another of Shover's informants explained:

> *"You get to thinking as you get older, you get wiser. You get to thinking there's no percentage in stealing because you can't constantly keep it up without getting caught and if you get caught, you're back in the penitentiary. And who wants to go back for five more years? . . . Now no amount of money is worth my freedom because too many things can happen, plus you're losing all the luxury of being free. You're locked up." (p. 140)*

A pattern of desisting from crime or engaging in less serious crimes was observed among the older, more experienced burglars in our research, and on the part of many who were interviewed but did not qualify as informants because they had retired or had reduced their activity level below that required by our operational definition of active burglars. Four of our informants were desisters at the time of the study. They had either terminated their criminal careers completely or had switched from burglary to "less serious" offenses such as shoplifting or fencing. Most of the remaining twenty-six informants had desisted at least once during their criminal careers. Among the desisters in our study, the decision to desist—to abandon a career as a burglar—often appeared to be the result of reappraisal of the costs and benefits of a criminal lifestyle. This reappraisal appeared to begin in the late twenties and early thirties for most of those we interviewed. In one case the burglar was over forty years

of age before deciding that life as a burglar was "too hard." In another, the burglar was only nineteen years of age when he made the decision to desist.

We found support for most of the aging-out theories among our informants. It appeared that the decision to desist or to substitute one criminal activity for another was an individual decision. For one, marriage and the acquisition of a family appeared to be the primary motivation. For others, desistance was a gradual process that appeared to be associated with the disintegration of the adolescent peer group, and with employment and the ability to earn money legitimately. One such informant said:

Used to be I spent all my time with my homies, you know, hanging out and partying—drinking beer and fuckin' around. Now, you know, with my new lady [wife], I gotta work—make some clean money. . . .Once you get in the groove it's [working's] not so bad and the best part is not havin' to look over your shoulder all the time.

Another explained that since he and his common-law wife had their first child, he had changed "overnight" into "a totally square dude." And another informant, a forty-five-year-old former burglar and shoplifter admitted:

Two things . . .one is that I can't do it anymore. I hurt my back once when I fell when I was trying to climb one of those concrete block fences behind this house I was doing. That getaway turned into a "crawl-away." I never been the same— physically, you know. Two is I don't get the same blast from it I used to. Used to get this adrenaline rush. Now, it's not that exciting.

For most of the desisters we interviewed, however, the final decision to terminate a criminal lifestyle was primarily the result of their increasing fear of punishment. In the early years of their criminal career, the informants stated that they did not perceive the criminal justice system as a deterrent to their criminal activities. The risk–gain calculus they employed when making decisions about criminal activity placed little weight on the probability of official sanctions. They were aware of the low apprehension rate for property crimes and believed the probability of being arrested for any specific crime was very small. Each active informant was asked, "For any particular burglary, what do you think are your chances of being caught?" Over 90 percent of the informants replied either "1 in 50" or "1 in 100." Their own arrest history confirmed and reinforced this perception. Thus, arrest appeared to be a negligible factor in their cost–benefit analysis.

Furthermore, most believed that even if they were arrested and convicted, they would be granted probation for the first conviction for burglary or other property crime. As one informant stated, "You get one free crime." The perception of probation as a free crime was widespread. As a sanction, probation was perceived as a suspended sentence with almost no negative consequences. The informants we interviewed regularly committed crimes and used drugs while on probation or parole. Few of them felt any serious pressure to cease or even reduce their criminal activities during their probationary period. The general perception was that probation and parole officers were overworked,

understaffed, and underfunded. The informants were asked if they had been required to submit to random drug screening during their term of probation or parole. Over 75 percent of those who were on probation or parole, or had previously been on probation or parole, stated they had not. Several stated that the probation or parole officer scheduled urine screening tests as much as thirty days in advance. This had the practical effect of allowing the probationer to "get clean" for the test or to avoid the test altogether. Most, however, had never been required to submit a urine sample for drug screening purposes. Others avoided urine testing by failing to show for scheduled tests or failing to make their regular report day whenever they suspected or were told by other probationers to expect a surprise urine screening. Few reported serious consequences as a result of their artifice. Probation officers were thought by the informants to be too busy to follow up on these evasions.

Although the risk side of the equation was perceived to be negligible because of the inadequacy of the criminal justice system, the gain or benefit side was enhanced by the excitement of crime, the monetary benefits of crime, and the association of crime and drug use (viewed as a pleasurable experience by most informants). Two principles of learning are that behaviors that are rewarded (reinforced) tend to recur, and behaviors that are punished are suppressed. To be effective as a suppressor, however, punitive consequences must be immediate, reasonably severe, and consistent (a sure thing).

Burglary provides many reinforcements to the participants. Our informants related numerous reward points during and after a burglary. On the other hand, punishments are few and intermittent. Burglars consistently reported committing fifty to 100 crimes before being apprehended and two to three times that many between periods of incarceration. Thus, whenever the cost–benefit analysis was employed, the gains and benefits were perceived to vastly outweigh the possible risks. However, like the subjects studied by Glassner and his associates (1983) and many of Shover's (1971, 1996) informants, there was a point in the careers of our informants at which the costs/risks appeared to be weighted more heavily. Although those who had served a short term of imprisonment (a year or less) did not often view the experience as particularly onerous, those who served longer sentences (defined by almost all as three to five years or more) felt the pains of imprisonment more surely. Many felt they could serve a year or two easily, but beyond that, the time was too "hard to do." One forty–three-year-old former burglar stated: "I can still do six months in county or even a year in the joint, but as I get older the time gets harder and harder to do. Didn't used to be. I could do a nickel [five years] with no sweat. Can't no more."

Another told us: "A year ain't no time. I can do that. I don't want to take no chances on having to serve five or six or seven years. That's more than I could do."

The pattern of desisting from crime or changing their predominant criminal activity to one less physically demanding, or one with less harsh penalties, was most readily apparent in the careers of those informants who had served at least one previous incarceration and who perceived that the next conviction

might carry a substantially longer term of imprisonment. Research appears to support this observation. In a study of 108,000 persons released from prisons in eleven states in 1983, the Bureau of Justice Statistics reported that prisoners who had served more than five years in prison had lower rates of re-arrest than other offenders (Beck, 1989).

Arturo, a desister for the three years previous to our interview, told us that not only would the sentences be longer because of his past record, but he would be placed in a more secure institution and would have difficulty making parole: "Automatically they would send me to a maximum security unit. The possibilities would be slim, because of my label [recidivist], that I would make parole."

The informants also perceived that the certainty of apprehension, conviction, and punishment increased after the first incarceration. Previous research on the deterrent effects of certainty and of severity of sanctions has found certainty to be more important than severity in producing conformity (Hawkins and Alpert, 1989; Tittle and Logan, 1973; Zimring and Hawkins, 1973). Tittle and Logan concluded that severity is associated with lower crime rates only at some levels of certainty. Data from the present study appear to support this hypothesis. Severity of punishment has little, if any, impact on the risk–gain calculus of the younger offender—until the probability of punishment becomes greater. The probability of being apprehended for a crime was judged by our informants to be greater as they became better known to the police. They believed that their modus operandi was more often recognized and that they were more likely to be considered possible suspects after a crime. Previously incarcerated burglars also viewed themselves as more likely to be convicted if apprehended. Prosecutors were perceived to be more likely to use previous convictions as leverage in plea bargaining. Previously convicted burglars are thus more likely to plead guilty and negotiate a sentence, knowing that if they go to trial and are convicted, the sentence will be much longer than one negotiated in advance. Benny, a journeyman burglar with two previous incarcerations, told us why he eventually gave up crime: "It got to where they come and got me every time something went down within five miles of my house. I was afraid of getting forty years or life or something."

Åkerström (1983) reported a similar finding: "The former thieves I have talked to often referred to the fact that at the end of their careers, they got caught too easily due to their records and the time inside tended to increase" (p. 203).

When long sentences began to seem inevitable, many of the older recidivist burglars in our study desisted or took up less serious crime. Some reported getting out of the criminal life entirely, or trying to. One informant told us: "I've been down twice before and the next one could be the "bitch" [life imprisonment as a habitual offender]. It's not worth it anymore."

A larger group reported that they began to participate in less serious crimes. Fearing the consequences of a new felony conviction, many began shoplifting—boosting—a misdemeanor in most jurisdictions. Arturo said: "I didn't want to get the bitch so I quite doing burglaries and started shoplifting."

Arturo, like many other burglars turned boosters, found that merchandise obtained through shoplifting was more easily converted to cash and more profitable than items obtained through burglary. Shoplifted items are new and usually have a price tag attached. They are easy to fence and the price is usually better than for used items taken in a burglary. Shoplifters can also attempt to obtain a refund from the store when the items are stolen, thus recouping 100 percent of the value instead of the 10 to 30 percent that they would receive from a fence. A conviction for shoplifting is also less likely to result in a prison sentence than a conviction for burglary.

This functional displacement into less serious criminal activity appears to result, at least in part, from the deterrent effect of fairly predictable apprehension, conviction, and longer sentences for previously convicted burglars, and from their perceptions of boosting as being a more cost effective, and less risky mode of criminal behavior. However, these findings conceivably may be an artifact of the sample selection, or of the local criminal culture. Rengert and Wasilchick (1989) found that burglars who were displaced from their usual activities tended to engage in more serious criminal activity, such as robbery. If, however, functional displacement is brought about by an assessment of the costs and risks of burglary compared to the potential rewards, then displacement into more serious criminal activity would not be a rational response.

The decision to terminate a criminal career or even to effect a career change (e.g., shoplifting instead of burglary) must be considered in relation to drug use by the offenders. All of our informants were drug addicts or regular users of illegal drugs. Terminating a criminal career would almost necessarily be associated with a change in drug use patterns.

We found that the cessation of the criminal career and drug use patterns tended to occur at the same time. We have previously proposed that criminal activity is rational behavior, such that the individual chooses criminal behavior after a rational assessment of the risks and costs of crime compared to the potential rewards. Bennett (1986) characterizes drug taking behavior as equally rational. He argues that offender choices and decisions govern in important ways the initiation, continuation, and cessation of drug use. He concludes that individuals desist from drug use for many of the same reasons as individuals who desist from other criminal activity. He concludes that situational factors such as a change of job or abode sometimes play a role in the addict's decision to desist from drug taking. Sometimes addicts simply tire of the lifestyle. In short, drug users are much more in control of their lives than previously thought.

SUMMARY

The rational choice perspective appears to be a useful way of understanding and analyzing not only the initiation of criminal behavior and drug taking, but also the cessation of these behaviors. Burglars reported desisting from crime or functionally displacing (to less serious types of crime such as

shoplifting) for a variety of reasons. Some simply appeared to "age out"—losing interest in the activities that excited and thrilled them when younger. Some gained powerful ties to conventional society through marriage or by obtaining a meaningful job, making burglary less attractive. Many others, however, desisted only after having served one or two previous incarcerations. These desisters reported that they had finally begun to consider the potential long-term consequences of their behavior. Their past criminal history made them more subject to increasingly severe penalties.

7

❖

Implications for
Prevention and
Public Policy

Crime prevention strategies based on rational choice theory assume that offenders freely and actively choose to commit crimes, basing their decisions upon a rational calculation of the costs and benefits associated with the behavior and arriving at a decision that maximizes gain (Bennett, 1986). Our findings support a limited rational choice model of criminal decision making and suggest that only in extreme cases are criminal events not characterized by at least limited rationality. The findings suggest that although offenders are not completely rational, they may usually be characterized as exercising some degree of decision making processing in choosing among alternative targets and deciding how and whether to effect entry. Most burglaries, however, do not result from a careful planning process or the use of sophisticated techniques. Unlike the economic model of crime that relies on the concept of maximization of outcomes, our limited rationality explanation of burglary rests on the assumption that burglars are seeking satisfactory target choices, not optimal ones. The decision model can best be characterized as a "satisficing" (Simon, 1982) strategy as opposed to an optimizing one. We found that most burglars are opportunists and respond primarily to cues in the physical environment that indicate immediate vulnerability and immediate risk. These opportunistic burglars do not heavily weigh long-term costs, risks, or benefits. To be effective, crime prevention strategies must consider this here-and-now orientation of the typical burglar.

A burglar is more likely to respond to crime prevention strategies at the neighborhood, block, or individual residence level than to those at the

community, state, or national level. Except under certain circumstances, crime prevention strategies at the community level, such as increased levels of prosecution, or at the state level, such as increasing statutory penalties for burglary, were not perceived by the informants as being as effective as micro-level strategies instituted by the residents of a potential target site, such as buying a dog or installing an alarm. Our informants appeared to be more concerned with the possibility of immediate detection and with immediate rewards. Crime prevention strategies that assign the risks and costs of burglary to the future (e.g., incarceration, after apprehension or after conviction) were viewed by most of our informants as almost hypothetical. With the exception of those burglars who had served one or more previous sentences, the potential for future punishment did not appear to deter them to any significant degree, undoubtedly because if punishment is rendered, it is long delayed. Rewards from crime, on the other hand, are numerous and immediate.

DRUGS AND CRIME PREVENTION

Any attempt to reduce the level of property crime must take into account its interdependence with drug use. Traditional wisdom assumes that unless demand for drugs is reduced (through education and treatment), supplies of drugs are interdicted (through vigorous law enforcement), or the use of drugs is legalized, the level of predatory property crime will continue to rise. Our research suggests, however, the possibility that drug use does not create an intractable impetus to crime. If addicts can, as our informants reported, control their intake, then crime prevention measures might have the effect of reducing both property crime rates and drug use. Except for extreme cases of imminent drug withdrawal, addicts will be deterred by the same strategies that deter other burglars.

Our research revealed numerous instances in which an addicted offender planned a burglary and was deterred temporarily by some situational factor, such as a neighbor watching the target house or the presence of a dog or an alarm system. Occasionally the deterred burglar located another burglary target and committed a burglary, as intended. Just as often, however, the planned crime was not committed and the potential burglar borrowed money, shoplifted, or sold something legitimately obtained. From a public policy perspective, each of these alternative courses of action is preferable to burglary. This is not to suggest that supply and demand strategies should be abandoned, however, rather that situational crime prevention measures might serve as an important adjunct to them.

Findings regarding mutual interdependence of drugs and property crime suggest that intervention strategies must target both behaviors. Drugs don't cause crime, they facilitate and reinforce it. Until the drug abuse aspect of property crime is adequately addressed, no intervention strategy will be effective in reducing the overall rate and incidence of property crime.

The research found that, at least in the jurisdiction studied, community correctional programs failed to screen property offenders aggressively for drug use. We believe that regular, random drug screening and drug treatment must be an essential component of any probation, parole, or pretrial services supervision plan. Most drug screening programs in criminal justice test only known or suspected users. Findings that indicate that two to four times more arrested offenders use drugs than are discovered by self-reports suggest that all pretrial releasees and all probationers be initially screened for drug use. In the case of new referrals, only when three to five random drug screenings have failed to show drug use should the screening requirement be reduced or eliminated. For those who are known drug users or those whose initial screenings give evidence of drug use, drug testing and treatment should be mandated for the entire term of supervision.

HINDERING CRIMINAL OPPORTUNITIES

In addition to employing situational property crime prevention measures and repeated drug screenings, the opportunity to commit property crime must be disrupted. Rengert and Wasilchick (1989) found that time was an important aspect in defining criminal opportunities. This is because specific sites are opportunities for burglary only at specific times of day when they are unoccupied or appear to the burglar to be unguarded or vulnerable. Burglaries require that the burglar's schedule and that of the victim coincide to leave the home vulnerable (Rengert and Wasilchick, 1989, p. 85). This means that if potential burglars are working at legitimate employment or attending school during most of the hours when most homes are most vulnerable (8:00 A.M. to 4:00 P.M.), their opportunities for criminal activity are restricted. The findings of the present study demonstrated that individuals could not easily hold a job and commit burglaries at the same time. Prime burglary hours are also prime working hours. We suggest implementation of sanctions that restrict the offenders' discretionary use of those time periods during which society is most at risk from residential property crime—the typical working day. Probation and parole conditions should mandate full daytime employment or some approved alternative, such as school or vocational training. Supervised restriction to the home (house arrest) might be required for those not working or not in school.

Job training or full employment policies in probation and parole programs in the past have not proven completely successful. This may be the result of the belief that offenders would work at legitimate employment if they were given the opportunity or were vocationally qualified. Rengert and Wasilchick write: "Many assume that employment provides an alternative income source to crime which nearly everyone would choose if given the opportunity. Our research demonstrates that all the individuals we studied had the chance to choose work over crime" (p. 110).

Without exception, the informants in the present study possessed the necessary skills and the opportunity to maintain regular employment. They chose not to work. Their drug use, partying, and criminal behavior patterns were not compatible with regular employment.

TARGETING THE FENCE

Cook (1989) has suggested looking to the economic paradigm as a means of analyzing crime. Marketing-oriented complexes of criminal activity undergird most forms of vice and theft. Therefore, it would be logical to apply this economic perspective in crime control—to develop a strategy to "guide the use of sanctions against the complex of activities that support a particular type of crime" (Cook, 1989, p. 68). He suggested that a thief-oriented enforcement strategy would be less effective than a comprehensive approach based on an understanding of the market for criminal activity. Any crime control measures that increase the cost/risk of doing business for the receivers of stolen property should reduce the profitability and therefore, ultimately, the volume of theft (Cook, 1989).

Law enforcement efforts in this domain are usually targeted toward the professional fence. It is true that targeting the professional fence may be more effective in reducing the incidence of theft than arresting several thieves. Thieves are "more readily replaceable" than those to whom they market their stolen merchandise (Cook, 1989, p. 70). We believe, however, that the professional fence represents a market for only 30 to 40 percent of all stolen property. Although professional fences exist and prosper, much stolen property is sold instead to ordinary, everyday, and otherwise honest citizens. Stuart Henry (1978) wrote: "Taken together these property crimes are a significant feature of modern life, comprising a *hidden economy* operating within the legitimate economy of society" (p. 5).

Although the extent to which ordinary citizens participate in the hidden economy is yet undetermined, our findings and those of Henry suggest that this part-time crime is ubiquitous. Unlike the professional fence, these individuals do not perceive themselves as criminal or as part of the impetus that drives property crime and drug sales. Yet, were it not for their willingness to purchase stolen property, the market for stolen goods might well shrink to less than one-half its current size. Furthermore, given that recent research has found that 60 to 90 percent of all burglars use illegal drugs and use the proceeds from their thefts to buy drugs, the amateur fence might also be characterized as a facilitator of drug abuse and drug sales, as well as of burglary and other forms of property crime. However, as Henry states, "Members of the hidden economy are rarely caught breaking the law, and even when they are, they are rarely sent through the criminal processing mill" (p. 13). The virtual lack of legal reaction and the carefree public attitude toward the fencing activity and those who engage in it tends to perpetuate and expand the behavior.

We suggest that failure to portray and to respond to fencing activity as an inextricable aspect of burglary, theft, shoplifting, and illicit drug sales allows the amateur and the avocational fence to maintain a self-image of respectability—even of being sharp businesspeople. Henry concluded: "Crucially important to their participation in trading activities is whether they can excuse, justify, rationalize or otherwise preserve their moral character, should their activities be subsequently questioned."

The amateur and avocational fences use a variety of rationalizations to maintain their self-image. Among them are: (a) "Everyone does it"; (b) "If I didn't, someone else would"; (c) "I didn't know for sure that it was stolen"; and (d) "No one was hurt but the insurance company." The failure of the criminal justice system to vigorously prosecute this part-time crime, or of society to condemn the activity, trivializes the behavior.

These relatively unstudied channels of redistribution of stolen property (amateur and avocational fences) may have important implications for crime prevention. Should crime prevention strategies circumscribe the market for stolen merchandise through prosecution of avocational and amateur fences, thieves would be forced to deal more frequently with professional receivers and would become more visible, because most professional fences are known to law enforcement. In addition, it is doubtful that the professional receivers would be able or willing to absorb the dramatic volume of stolen property currently being successfully redistributed through amateur fences. This market glut and the increased risks and costs to the professional receiver would probably lower the incidence of property crime. Finally, entry into the criminal work force by young and inexperienced thieves might be delayed or prevented if they failed to locate a ready market for their product. Thus, enforcement strategies targeting amateur and avocational fences could possibly decrease the incidence of property theft. By increasing the risks and costs to professional fences and the thieves with whom they deal, such strategies would serve as an economic deterrent to property theft.

Although broad-reaching crime control strategies such as we have suggested above are critical to the long-term reduction in burglary and other property crimes, developing individual burglary prevention techniques are also among the goals of this study. As Cornish and Clarke (1986) assert, if one perceives offenders as relentless in their search for targets and victims, then little can be done to prevent crime, except long-term, often fruitless efforts to change or rehabilitate. Research has often failed to produce empirical support for treatment-oriented paradigms of crime prevention, deterrence, or rehabilitation (Cornish and Clarke, 1986; Martinson, 1974; Lipton, Martinson and Wilks, 1975). Recent years have witnessed a resurgence of interest in an alternative perspective to crime prevention strategies based on rational choice theory. As discussed more fully in earlier chapters, rational choice theory in criminology assumes that rewards and punishments influence the offender's decision to offend or to refrain from offending. Our study clearly supports a limited rational choice perspective on offending. Time and again the burglar subjects advanced *choice* as their motivation for committing criminal acts.

Asked why they offended, their most common response was, "I needed (or wanted) money".

Based on these findings and those of others (Wright and Decker, 1994; Shover, 1996; Jacobs and Wright, 1999), we conclude that prevention strategies that emphasize reducing opportunities for offending have the greatest utility for successful burglary reduction. Although most burglars are opportunistic, they are nonetheless, at least to some degree, rational, making use of environmental cues at or near the proposed target site. The evidence suggests that even though there are no foolproof ways to protect a home from burglars, a few simple precautions will reduce vulnerability. They are designed to cause a potential burglar to perceive a target site as too risky and/or offering too meager a reward for the effort and risk involved.

Two prevention strategies that focus on reduction of criminal opportunities are *Situational Crime Prevention* (Clarke, 1997) and *Crime Prevention through Environmental Design* (Jeffery, 1971). These two prevention strategies are very similar, however Situational Crime Prevention (SCP) is most effective at the micro-level—that is, at the target site—a home or a business location. Crime Prevention through Environmental Design (CPTED) is a macro-level strategy, most effective at the street, neighborhood, or community level. Both can be effective opportunity reduction methods.

SITUATIONAL CRIME PREVENTION

Situational Crime Prevention (SCP) is a crime-specific strategy. It focuses on a narrow range of criminal behavior. That is, an SCP technique might be designed to reduce convenience store robberies, or car burglary, or to reduce store theft. SCP focuses more on efforts by businesses and individuals than it does on the police or other formal agencies of social control. SCP approaches prevention through four general strategies:

- Increasing the risk to the potential offender
- Increasing the effort required to commit the crime
- Reducing the reward
- Removing excuses

The first three of these have value in individual or micro-level prevention. Increasing the risk involves such techniques as formal and informal surveillance. Formal surveillance may be accomplished through the use of security guards, police patrol, burglar alarms, security cameras, improved lighting, and neighborhood watch. Informal surveillance involves creating a physical environment that promotes the ability of neighbors and passersby to observe the site. Trimming shrubs and other landscaping to minimize hiding places is one method of facilitating informal surveillance. Increasing the effort involves target hardening strategies such as dead-bolt locks, fenced yards, gated communities, and building homes on cul-de-sacs. Reducing the reward may

be accomplished by not keeping valuable items in the home and marking property for identification.

Removing excuses recognizes that ". . . offenders make judgments about the morality of their own behavior and that they frequently rationalize or neutralize what would otherwise be incapacitating feelings of guilt or shame through such excuses as 'He deserved it,' 'I was just borrowing it,' and 'I only slapped her'" (Clarke, 1997, p.16). The control of disinhibitors such as drugs and alcohol fall into this category.

Increase the Risk to the Offender

The most important ingredient of increasing risk in a situational crime prevention approach to burglary is to give a residence the illusion of occupancy. Nearly all burglars will avoid an occupied residence (see also Wright and Decker, 1994). The most important of all the steps the burglar takes in arriving at a decision to break into a targeted residence is to determine his level of risk, and the issue of whether or not anyone is at home is at the heart of that assessment. There are many cues that point to a site as occupied or unoccupied. The usual advice for residents leaving town on vacation is to enlist someone to pick up the newspapers and mail, or to stop the paper and mail delivery altogether. That is good advice, but it is not sufficient. Burglars look for lawns that are not mowed, the absence of the boat or cars from the driveway, and lights, particularly outdoor lights, kept on all day and all night.

The burglars in the study suggested the following steps by which a house may be made to seem occupied:

1. Install a telephone answering machine that answers within two rings and responds with either a message that implies that the resident stepped out for a few minutes and will be right back, or a message that implies that someone is home but the phone is rarely answered in person. If the resident is a single female, she should have a male voice make the outgoing recording using the word "we" instead of "I."

2. Do not put a name on the mailbox or anywhere outside the home. Burglars often read a name on a mailbox, note the address, and simply go to a phone book and get the number from the directory. They then dial the number from the nearest phone booth (or cell phone), put the phone down, and return to the door or window. If they hear the telephone still ringing, they know that no one is home. Permanent slot-type mail boxes where the mail drops through the door or wall, or U.S. Postal Service Centralized Mail Delivery boxes, are recommended over curbside boxes. They prevent the burglar from using mail left in the mailbox as a cue to determine whether anyone is at home and they prevent easy access to telephone numbers.

3. Install inexpensive timers (about $10) on normally used interior and exterior lights so they turn on and off at normal times. An outside light left on all day or an inside light burning all night is a sure tip-off of absence.

4. Put a radio or TV on a timer, too, and have it playing loud enough to be heard from outside the front door or window. Set the timer to play a radio from morning to bedtime. The TV is better in the evening. Put the TV in a room with a window to the outside and pull the blinds or curtains. An observer outside may confuse the flickering caused by the TV's ever-changing brightness with human movement on the inside.

5. Leave a car in the driveway or in front of the house. As a habit, park it in various locations about the house from day to day. If away on a trip, ask a neighbor to move your car daily from one parking spot to another, or to park his car in your driveway when coming to and from work.

6. Ask a neighbor to leave a bag or can of garbage at your house on regular collection days.

7. Ask a friend or neighbor to enter your house twice daily, once in the morning and again about dusk. It is a good idea to open the curtains, blinds, and shutters a bit in the morning and then close them in the evening.

8. Install outdoor floodlights and have them on a timer, too. They should be set to come on before dusk and go off after sunrise.

In other words, even though no one is in the house, it can give the illusion of occupancy, thus causing it to be perceived by the burglar as too risky.

After burglars have satisfied themselves that the potential target site is unoccupied, the next step to be determined is whether neighbors or other persons will see them as they case the site and commit the burglary. Consequently, one effective prevention strategy is composed of "nosy neighbors"—alert and vigilant persons who know their neighborhood and know the habits of those who live nearby. Nosy neighbors recognize strangers and know who has business being on the block. They exercise prudent guardianship by watching out for themselves and their fellow residents.

One informant, twenty-three years of age, who has been a burglar for seven years and arrested only once, told us that the thing she feared the most was "old people." She stated that neighborhoods with a predominance of elderly or retired persons were on her "no-hit" list. She said: "These people are nosy. They watch out for strangers and they call the police. I stay away from neighborhoods where old people live."

This female burglar expanded her "no-hit" list to include neighborhoods with children playing in yards and houses with noisy dogs. Children tend to be territorial, and they notice strangers. Daytime burglars depend on being overlooked and will usually move on if they attract any attention. Noisy dogs are also unsettling. Dogs attract attention with their barking and they bark most often at strangers. They call attention to the burglar studying a potential target and cause the would-be burglar to feel less secure working in that neighborhood. Nosy humans and noisy dogs are primary components of a successful burglary prevention strategy. This technique of watchfulness and guardianship, and reporting suspicious behavior to police, underlies crime

prevention programs such as Neighborhood Watch. In a British burglary study (Forrester, Chatterton and Pease, 1988), two factors were found to discriminate between victimized residences and neighboring nonvictimized residences—the presence of a dog and signs of occupancy. At the time of the burglary, 42 percent of victimized houses were said to look occupied. In contrast, 80 percent of the neighboring houses appeared occupied.

Next to nosy neighbors and noisy dogs, the most effective means of increasing the risk for the burglar is installing a security system. We found that only the most professional burglars were willing to take on a house with a burglar alarm. In the British study above (Forrester et al., 1988), burglars indicated that alarm systems were among the factors considered most risky. Over one-half stated that they would not burglarize a residence with a visible alarm system. The burglars in our study reported greater levels of deterrence with regard to alarms. While many burglars stated that they were not deterred by alarms, when we asked them to compare vulnerable and nonvulnerable sites, none of the subjects rated an alarmed residence as vulnerable. Rather, they appeared to accept a yard or window sign indicating that an alarm was present as proof that it existed. In their study of 105 burglars in St. Louis, Wright and Decker arrived at similar conclusions regarding the deterrent value of alarms, stating:

> Most offenders . . . wanted to avoid alarms all together, and upon encountering such devices, abandoned all thought of attacking the dwelling. Indeed, 56 of the 86 subjects we questioned about this issue, said that they were not prepared to burglarize an alarmed residence under any circumstances. (p. 125)

One of the most interesting findings of the research was the value of privacy fences—to the burglar, that is! Most of the homes in the area studied had six- to eight-foot-high wood or masonry fences enclosing the backyard. These fences afford residents privacy for outdoor activities, and they allow the burglar the same protection from prying eyes. Replacing a privacy fence with a chain-link fence, or lowering the wooden fence to a maximum height of four feet, may be one of the best tactics an individual can employ to reduce the probability of becoming a burglary victim.

Increase the Effort for the Burglar

Burglars follow the route of least resistance, almost always choosing a target that is easy to get into over one that appears difficult. Although it is virtually impossible to make a residence burglar proof, residents can make entry more difficult or more time-consuming. One effective way to make entry more difficult is to install dead-bolt or vertical-bolt locks, and metal doors and doorjambs. Research on the efficacy of security hardware for burglary prevention is less consistent than for alarms, dogs, and occupancy. However, with few exceptions (but see Wright and Decker), researchers have merely recorded the burglars' responses to questions about dead-bolt locks and other target hardening devices, without actually testing their answers against actual

practices. Findings from our study and from some prior research (Wright and Decker) indicate that security hardware such as locks on doors and windows does deter many burglars. The burglars in our study had a general rule of thumb: "If it takes more than two minutes to get in, forget it." Although even the best locks and doors will not stop a determined thief, they are obstacles that require time and noise to circumvent. The best locks in the world, however, are of no value if not used. Our informants estimated that doors and windows were not locked in over one-half the houses they entered.

Reduce the Reward

Conspicuous displays of affluence increase a dwelling's attractiveness as a burglary target. Expensive jewelry, guns, art, and antiques on display in a home when repairmen, salesmen, deliverymen, and other strangers may be coming and going is an invitation to burglars who are constantly on the lookout for opportunity. Jewelry and other valuable small items, such as coin and stamp collections, should be stored in a safe deposit box. Publicity or casual talk about collections of guns, coin collections, or other hobbies might tip off a burglar that a home contains valuable items. The greater the potential payoff, the more risks the burglar will take to obtain it.

None of these situational crime prevention strategies will guarantee that an individual will not be a burglary victim, but they should significantly reduce the odds of victimization.

CRIME PREVENTION THROUGH ENVIRONMENTAL DESIGN (CPTED)

Crime Prevention through Environmental Design (CPTED) is a crime prevention strategy that is in many ways like Situational Crime Prevention. Both involve manipulating the physical and social environment to reduce opportunities for crime. Where SCP tends to be most effective at the actual crime site, such as at a residence, business location, or small public area, CPTED usually operates at the block, neighborhood, or community level. CPTED also involves a broader spectrum of criminal behavior. Where SCP can be implemented at specific sites by individuals (installing locks, building fences, placing valuable property in a safe deposit box), CPTED is generally less capable of being employed by individuals and less easily retrofitted. CPTED techniques are best developed at the planning and design stage.

The basic tenet of CPTED is that proper design and effective use of the built environment can reduce the fear and incidence of crime and thereby improve the overall quality of life (Jeffery, 1971; Crowe and Zahm, 1994). CPTED emphasizes three design approaches:

- Access control
- Natural surveillance
- Territoriality

Access control involves doors, gates, shrubbery, fences, and other physical features to limit access to all but intended users. *Natural surveillance* is achieved by placement of windows and other openings in locations that allow users to see and be seen as they engage in their routine activities. Surveillance is enhanced by appropriate lighting and landscaping. *Territoriality* suggests that people will protect and defend space that they occupy. Increasing territorial behavior is achieved by use of sidewalks, landscaping, and other elements that distinguish between public and private areas.

These three environmental design approaches comprise burglary prevention strategies using CPTED principles.

Access Control

Access control involves locks and other target hardening techniques, as well as general design elements such as gated communities, street closures, fences, and certain landscaping features. Access control facilitates the offender's perception of risk, slowing and restricting their activities, and subjecting them to higher levels of surveillance. Research has demonstrated that neighborhoods that are harder to drive through have less crime than those that are more permeable (Cisneros, 1995). Our research also found that the more restrictive the access to a residence, the less likely it will be burglarized. Houses on cul-de-sacs will have lower burglary rates than those on through-streets. Houses on corners have higher burglary rates than those in the middle of the block.

Landscaping can also provide access control, creating real or symbolic barriers. Many plants and shrubs, such as roses, bougainvillea, holly, and pyracantha, bear thorns and may be used to make access to otherwise vulnerable windows uncomfortable, even dangerous to the burglar.

Natural Surveillance

In order to defend property, the individual must be able to see illegal activity as it occurs. Activities that make the offender more likely to be seen reduce the likelihood of crime. Burglars repeatedly reported that one of their major concerns was to remain unseen and thus unreported. Heavy shrubbery near doors and windows, blind corners, and windows and doors that are not overlooked by neighbors or passersby, and "privacy," and "privacy" fences all facilitate burglary. Conversely, entrance and egress points that are clean and open and easily visible from the street or neighbors' homes reduce the burglars' crime opportunities.

Most persons who are attempting to "burglar-proof" their homes add improved outdoor lighting. While well-lit areas do tend to deter nighttime burglars, it should be noted that 60 to 80 percent of all residential burglaries occur during daylight hours. However, a small, but significant percentage of burglaries do occur at night and various other criminal activities, such as vandalism, assault, and rape are more prevalent after dark. Homeowners should maintain a well-lit premises and seek high quality street lighting in their neighborhoods. Darkness makes police, passersby and neighbors less likely to

observe criminal behavior. Darkness and shadows provide good cover for watching a potential burglary target and covering a burglar's escape.

Territoriality

A space that is well maintained appears to be "owned" and will discourage illegitimate or disruptive users and will encourage territorial behavior by residents (Kelling and Coles, 1996). We found that well maintained homes and yards create a perception in the minds of potential burglars that this property will be defended. One burglar asserted: "Those people take good care of their place. Mowing and edging and keeping everything so neat and clean. They probably got alarms and stuff if they think like that and keep the place so neat."

Another stated: "No! I wouldn't do that house at all. No way. It's too nice. Everybody in this neighborhood be outside all the time working in the yard and talking to each other. They looking out for their place."

Improving the appearance of the environment, particularly the home and yard, but more widely, the block and neighborhood tend to promote territorial behavior on the part of residents. Personalizing the environment by planting flower beds, and shrubs and hedges along property lines also provide a delineation between public and private property while sending a message of ownership and guardianship. Increasing territoriality is also enhanced through social activities as Neighborhood Watches and "Nights Out Against Crime" programs.

SUMMARY

Burglary prevention must be addressed both at the public policy level as well as the individual site level. Policies that impact drug and alcohol use and control, the market for stolen goods, and improving community corrections' ability to monitor and supervise those under their care are critical reduction strategies. Burglary prevention also must be addressed both at the individual target site level and at the street, neighborhood, and community level. Situational crime prevention techniques are most effective for protecting the individual home and surrounding property. SCP is crime specific. The techniques we have suggested here focus on protecting the individual from burglary. CPTED provides a "shell" of protection, making the larger environment less susceptible to criminal activity in general. Together they reduce criminal opportunities and provide a measure of safety and security by creating a perception in the minds of potential offenders that this neighborhood, block, or single residence represents too great a risk to those who might contemplate criminal activity.

Our findings tend to support the general hypothesis that a rational, hierarchal, sequential decision-making process could not adequately explain a substantial amount of the variance in burglary. We agree with Zajonc's (1980) conclusions that decision making has aspects of both cognitive and affective processes and that a model of behavior must accommodate both. A crime

prevention strategy that does not take into account the large percentage of burglars who use drugs and how drug use affects decision making, as well as the influence of co-actors on the decision process, will be ineffective.

A cognitive–behavioral analysis of subroutines, one that takes into account drug and group effects within the larger template model, may serve as the most fertile paradigm with which to examine the burglar's decision-making process and to design and implement crime prevention strategies.

Appendix A

Biographies of Selected Informants

The brief biographies that follow are generally representative of the informants in the study. The names used here are fictitious.

ROBERT

Robert is a professional burglar. He was born in Austin, Texas, in 1950. He graduated from high school in 1968 and was subsequently drafted into the Army, but opted to enlist in the Navy. He claims to have served two tours of duty with the Special Forces in Vietnam. He states that he received three Bronze Stars and a combat action award. When he returned home in 1973, he said: "It didn't mean anything to anybody and I couldn't get my old job back as a welder. Burglary was so easy."

He pulled his first burglary three months after returning home. In the years that followed he became a skilled and respected burglar. His specialty was lake cottages and vacation houses within a ninety-mile radius of Austin.

Robert differed from the less professional burglars in our sample in several ways. First, his targets were always located far from his personal residence. Robert told the interviewer: "I take my van up to the lakes—sometimes a hundred miles from here. These houses are vacation homes. Sometimes the owner won't come back for a month or two, especially in the winter. I took air conditioners, everything I could fit into the van."

Robert did not learn burglary from other burglars. He told us:

The military taught me what I needed to know as a burglar. Planning, that's what I learned in the Army. Laying out a map in your head, getting it all together, and knowing who you're going to unload the stolen goods on before doing anything is also important. I guess my training in the Special Forces taught me to be sneaky and to rehearse things in my mind ahead of time because, you know, you're scared. The military taught me to have confidence in myself.

Finally, Robert was master of the ruse. All the burglars we worked with had developed probes to determine occupancy and the potential for the target site to be seen from other houses. Robert was an actor, having a varied routine to fit any occasion. Asked to describe examples of such probes, Robert answered:

Oh, I've got all kinds of ways to determine if somebody is at home. I might put on decent but not real outstanding clothes, and come out and do an acting routine. Looking down at my clipboard, I'd go up and knock on the door. I'm looking for a certain house, you know, and in case somebody is looking from across the street, I've opened the screen door with my foot to make it look like I'm talking with somebody. I'll move my arms half-pointing and say, "Okay, I'll go around to the back." Or, after knocking and nobody comes, I'll turn the doorknob. A lot of houses aren't locked. So I'll just walk in. Anybody who's watching thinks I've been asked inside by the owner.

Like every burglar in the study, Robert abused drugs and alcohol. Unlike most others, however, his drug of choice was methamphetamine—speed. He began injecting methamphetamine daily during his third year as a burglar. He stated that as he increased his speed use, he became sloppy as a burglar. He said that he was no longer professional about the selection of target sites nor about the distribution of the stolen merchandise. Once during this period Robert was high on methamphetamine and reported:

I'm talking about a house where there was a padlock on the back door and no vehicles around. Man, it looked liked nobody was there. When I got in I could smell smoke and I walked around. I opened the bedroom door to look in and see a fireplace going and a guy with this girl. I should have spotted that smoke coming out of the chimney and blown off the place.

Robert generally worked alone. There were occasions, however, when he needed help: either for assistance (to carry off very heavy items) or for "another pair of eyes" to watch for returning occupants. When he needed help he would invariably select a partner who had done "hard time" before, believing that such a person could not afford to be caught again. Robert also preferred partners on speed as opposed to heroin, saying: "A heroin addict will turn you in just to get his other shot, but a speed freak is not going to. He's too scared. A heroin addict you can't trust. A speed freak is too paranoid to turn you over."

He has recently reduced his drug use and has returned to his previous professional level skill and planning. He still uses speed; however, he claims to abstain when planning and executing burglaries.

He claims to have burglarized more than 2,000 dwellings during an eight-year period ending in 1981, when, after plea bargaining, he pleaded guilty to fifty-one counts of residential burglary. He subsequently served four years, nine months of a five-year sentence in the state prison.

ARTURO

Arturo is a former professional burglar, having been "clean" for several years. He is forty-one years old and is the oldest of five children. He began his criminal activity at age fourteen. Arturo's parents are still living and in their early sixties. Arturo's father no longer claims him as a son because of his past life as a criminal and drug addict. His mother continues to support him and wrote weekly during each period of incarceration. Arturo reports that his chief regret in his life is that his drug use and criminal activity destroyed his mother's life. He states that he is committed to straightening out, for both himself and to "make my mother proud of me for once." Arturo's father earned a modest living and the family was never on assistance. His mother never worked outside the home. Neither parent speaks English well and they live in an exclusively Hispanic neighborhood. Although Arturo dropped out of school in the ninth grade, he is intelligent, perceptive, and articulate. He attributes this to being a voracious reader while in prison with "endless hours without anything to do."

He began his criminal career while in junior high school, primarily because of his association with a sixteen-year-old friend who had been confined to youth detention centers for various offenses. He eventually became a part of a group of five boys who did burglary and shoplifting. They used the proceeds of their delinquent activity to purchase alcohol and marijuana. Arturo didn't enjoy marijuana, however, and immediately began experimentation with speed, quaaludes, LSD, and finally heroin. Arturo believes he became addicted after a year of what he terms infrequent use—administering only on weekends. His burglary activity increased to support his heroin habit. He dropped out of school, and shoplifting and burglary became his occupation. Except for a four-month stint in the prison bakery he never worked in a conventional job. Arturo reports never being convicted as a juvenile, although he was arrested three times. Each time he refused to confess and was released as a result of insufficient evidence. As an adult, Arturo was convicted three times and spent a total of thirteen years, eight months in the Texas prison system. His first incarceration, for possession, resulted in a seven-year sentence. He served five years, ten months. His behavior was erratic and netted him solitary confinement on four occasions. He was released and went to El Paso, where a friend and criminal associate lived. They began burglarizing and shoplifting. When the law "got close" on one occasion they moved to Mesa, Arizona, continuing their criminal activity.

After a year they returned to Odessa. After being out of prison about three and a half years, Arturo was again convicted for burglary after a co-offender gave him up in exchange for a probated sentence. Arturo is philosophical about the incident. Although he asserts that he wouldn't, "rat," "rat" on a partner, he stated that he was not in his "partner's shoes" and will not judge him. Arturo began his second incarceration with an aggressive, wild attitude and had long months of unpleasant physiological and psychological heroin withdrawal symptoms. Fights and failure to follow prison rules resulted in frequent and extended periods in solitary confinement. During this incarceration he read constantly and significantly increased his vocabulary, as well as improving his criminal expertise by association with other inmates. He served four years, ten months of the ten-year sentence. Upon release, his aunt and sister paid to send him to a private drug rehabilitation center in El Paso, which, after three months, proved fruitless. He returned to Odessa—and his association with his lifelong friend and co-offender—and began a very active phase of burglary, check forgery, and fencing stolen property for other offenders. Arturo was notorious among law enforcement as well as businessmen and store security personnel. His infamy was so pervasive that he is still, after ten years, not allowed in certain stores.

He remained "outside" for two and a half years, then was convicted on two counts of burglary. This third incarceration began like the others, but on his thirty-fifth birthday he decided he needed to "do something with his life" and had to get straight. He served three years of his sentence, receiving time for good behavior, and has remained clean since his release.

He is employed as a machinist, does volunteer work with drug addicts, and moonlights as a carpenter and general handyman. His association with all his friends and previous co-offenders has stopped, except for those who have stopped drug usage. Due to his vast experience as a burglar and his intimate knowledge of the criminal community in the area, Arturo served as a "consultant" to the study, often assisting us in determining the validity of information supplied to us by other informants.

DONNA

Donna is a white, forty-three-year-old professional burglar and heroin addict. She grew up in a lower-middle-class family. Both of her parents are living and are still married to one another. Her father has become moderately wealthy, having invested in oil leases and wells over the years. She reports that as a youngster her friends were "pimps, whores, and thieves." Donna dropped out of high school when she was sixteen years old and married when she was nineteen. Her first and only marriage lasted five years, until her husband was sent to prison for armed robbery. Since she was eighteen years old she has lived on the edge, supporting her marriage and herself through theft, burglary, shoplifting, and prostitution. She has "slowed down" over the past several years and now works occasionally for her father, who encourages her participation in a methadone maintenance program.

Donna's husband was twenty when she married him. She had never stolen until she met him. He served as her mentor in crime. They lived lavishly on the proceeds of their burglaries and armed robberies. She claims to have been "written up in the *Police Gazette*" during the heyday of her criminal activities.

She participated in her first burglary with her husband. She related: "The first one we did was a place out in the country. We knew they weren't there. I stood outside with a shotgun and I guess I would have shot rather than let my husband get caught. My job was to always stand watch with a shotgun."

In just the past three years she estimates she has participated in more than 200 to 300 burglaries—much more than she ever did when she was younger. She usually works with a male partner, but she breaks in, scans the rooms, and carries out as much as anyone. Sometimes she even works alone.

Donna likes to have inside information about the potential contents of a house before she burglarizes it. She states that she acquires such information by listening to people talk in restaurants and bars. She reports that she spends some mornings waiting at mall entrances/exits until a woman wearing expensive jewelry exits. She then follows the individual home. She reconnoiters the residence and returns later to burglarize it. She says:

So I drive by the front and back, looking for alarms that might go off. It was a lot easier over twenty-something years ago. A lot easier. Just sit and watch. Then go up to the front door and knock. If no one answers, then go in. But back then, see, they didn't have all these alarms, motion sensors and heat sensors and stuff. When I drive by I pay more attention to the back—I look for a sliding glass door. If it doesn't look like it has an alarm setup of any type I'll come back that afternoon or the next morning. If the car is gone I go up and knock on the front door. Oh, if someone were to answer the door, you know, I say, "Pardon me, is Mr. Brown in? . . . Mr. Jennings?" Mister anything, anybody I know. If they say, "No, you've got the wrong house," I act confused and say, "I'm sorry, thank you."

During the twenty years that Donna has been addicted to heroin she has never been drug free for more than a two-month period. Even now, she supplements her methadone with one to five papers (about $20 per paper) of heroin a day. For a recent three-month period when she was speed-balling—using cocaine and heroin at the same time—her habit ran $200 to $300 per day. In describing the many mornings when she'd wake up sick, having no heroin immediately at her disposal, she said:

Oh, I liked to use [heroin] before I would go and do a burglary, but I wasn't high, high, high, you know. I would have maybe fixed one or two papers to take the sick off then go to work [burglary]. You know, it's [heroin] a 24-hour-a-day problem. It doesn't go away. And then I'll go to work. But I'll do things that I wouldn't normally or ordinarily do when I'm sick. When I'm not sick, I'll stop and think a lot more. When I'm sick, I'll tend to hog anything I can, whether it be a house, a trailer. . . . I've gone into department stores and reached across the jewelry and watch counters and gotten stuff. I'm going to get it one way or another. I take greater risks when I'm sick.

When things got "too hot" for burglary Donna would turn to shoplifting—boosting. She had developed a reputation as a formidable booster, such that each Christmas season people would come to her with their requests. She'd carry a notebook and fill their Christmas shopping lists, Donna commented:

Now, because they do so much hard time for burglary and stuff, you'll find a lot of professional burglars that are tired of doing hard time and so a lot of them are into boosting. But you need customers for that, because, well, say you go into a department store for instance. You go in there and just start grabbing and then you have to drive around everywhere to unload it. You got to have some people that want that stuff and want it now. I'll fill your order whether it's a dress, a camera, a Rolex, or a carton of cigarettes!

Donna also turns to boosting when she is extremely sick. Boosting is preferred during such times because it's a quicker way to get cash or turn merchandise for drugs: "You can run into a convenience store, get four cartons of cigarettes and you've got a 'paper.' Or you can go into any supermarket and get five or six packages of ribeye steaks. I can unload the steaks in ten minutes."

GERALD

Gerald is twenty-two years old and a journeyman burglar. He was born in El Paso, Texas. Gerald's criminal life began early. He was eleven years old and living in Roswell, New Mexico, when his father left home. Soon afterward he broke into a neighborhood house with three other boys, all eleven years of age. They stole jewelry and money. The boys soon discovered there was money in burglary and decided to ride their bikes to what they called the "rich part of town." The four of them rode to the north side of town and hid their bikes in a field near a middle-class housing area. They walked for several blocks, finally finding a house that looked empty and burglarized it. Gerald commented retrospectively: "We did it, got away with it, and liked it. We thought it was great. We spent the money on video games."

In that first year, Gerald and his friends broke into fifteen to twenty homes; always at night. They always traveled by bicycle, but if the stolen merchandise was larger or heavier than they could carry on a bike, they would hide it and come back the next day in an older friend's car and pick it up.

When he was sixteen he was coached by two friends who were eighteen. They showed him how to disconnect alarms, open sliding patio doors, and other "tricks of the trade." The mentors burglarized only during the daytime. They taught Gerald how to sit patiently and "scope out a house," noting the time people left and returned and the whereabouts of others in the neighborhood. Gerald would sit in his car up the street about a half block and just watch. He was breaking into up to three houses per week during one period with his older friends.

Gerald was nine years old when he first experimented with marijuana, but it wasn't until he was fourteen years old that he became a frequent user. He reports that after age sixteen, he was always high on marijuana when he did

burglaries. To this day he continues to get high on marijuana before breaking into a house or apartment. He commented: "When I'm on that high I don't worry about no fear. I don't have no fear in me. I feel more calmed about myself and I can think pretty clear when I'm high."

At eighteen, he began using cocaine once or twice per week. He used cocaine in addition to marijuana and alcohol. He prefers primos, marijuana joints sprinkled with cocaine.

Gerald was most active as a burglar between the ages of eighteen and nineteen. During this period he committed burglaries mostly to obtain money to buy cocaine. He states that before cocaine, he did burglaries to party and to support his car and girlfriends. Although he claims never to be anything more than a weekly user of cocaine, obtaining it appears to have driven many of his burglaries.

Gerald has been arrested numerous times and has been convicted twice—once for possession of marijuana and on another occasion for burglary. He received probation both times. He successfully completed both terms of probation, although he states that he continued to use drugs and to commit burglaries while under supervision.

JERRY

Jerry is a journeyman burglar, the oldest son of a family of five children. Born and reared in west Texas, he lacks a year's worth of senior credits toward a bachelor's degree in business administration. His father left the family when Jerry was fourteen years old. His mother continued working as a maid but could barely make ends meet. Jerry is a heroin addict. He began as a burglar when he was eighteen years old, just after graduating from high school. He learned the essential skills of a burglar from a friend who was eighteen years old and always seemed to have a lot of money. Jerry liked the way he was doing things, and just "took up with him." This friend began showing Jerry what he had been doing to get money. At first, Jerry stood watch at target sites. Usually they'd enter through the rear alley and either jump the backyard fence or merely open the back gate. Jerry would watch the front street from the side of the house, just behind the fence. Jerry stated:

I'd get to where I could see the street and where my buddy could hear me. When we got in the house we would open the back door so we could have a way out. I'd watch. If I saw someone coming I'd go to the door and call him. I'd either whistle or holler and he would come out. If he needed me to help him with something heavy he would call me and I would go in. Most people will not come through the alley. Policemen won't come through the alley unless there was a report. So you don't have to watch the alley. They just patrol the streets; most of the time just the main streets. And if you watch them long enough you can tell which way they are going to go and when, 'cause they go almost the same way all the time.

Jerry and his friend continued doing night burglaries only, preferring the early evening. They burglarized houses in the neighborhood within about a

one-mile radius of their own home. They claimed to burglarize only places where they knew the occupants and knew where they had gone. Thus they tended to know what was in the house.

Although Jerry's drug of choice during this period was marijuana, he reports never stealing for drugs. He reports stealing "just for the money," and continues: "Anything you want, money could give it to you: cars, girls. You never keep any of this money. You never save any of this money. You don't, say, invest any of this money. The more money you make, the more you're just going to mess off."

After beginning to use, and becoming addicted to, heroin at age thirty-one, Jerry began to use the proceeds from his crimes to buy heroin. He claims to have little disposable income now; instead he uses almost all of his money to maintain his heroin habit.

He reported that he was always cautious to "fit in" a neighborhood. When casing an affluent white neighborhood, Jerry states: "During the day I have no reason to be there. If I could get some lawn mowers I'd have a reason to be out there. I need a reason to be there. At night I have no reason to be out there. That area, I stay away from. I work in mixed areas where blacks, whites, and Mexicans would stay."

He was married when he was twenty and soon afterward began a streak of four arrests for burglary for which he was not convicted. Then, when he was twenty-one he was arrested the fifth time. This time it was on ten counts of burglary and one count of armed robbery. As before, the burglary charges were dropped because of a lack of evidence, but because he was personally identified in the armed robbery, Jerry said "I just couldn't beat that." Jerry spent the next five years in prison. During this period his wife divorced him but he took college classes and earned his Associate of Arts degree. After leaving prison he remained in the free world for eight years, working primarily in construction and intermittently taking more college courses. He married a second time. At age thirty-four he was convicted and served another five-year term in prison for delivery of a controlled substance. As with the first, his second wife divorced him while in prison.

He has been arrested for burglary eight times but never convicted of that offense. Presently he is on parole and continuing to commit burglaries and to buy and sell heroin. He is receiving a small monthly check from an insurance settlement. He stated:

I know it's going to run out sooner or later. I have a little extra money coming in too, and that's why I don't do much burglary now. 'Course, you don't have to do as much as you did then to make $200. Fifteen years ago you had to do more burglaries. See, back then there wasn't a lot of merchandise like there is now. See, you wouldn't have to do three burglaries now because you have VCRs. Back then, you go in a house and get probably a TV. Maybe food. Now you can count on making much more per house for sure: a TV, VCR, microwave, watches, jewelry, and any money that's in the house.

Note: Shortly before this book went to press, Jerry was found dead in a ditch, the apparent victim of a gang slaying.

MARK

Mark is a journeyman burglar, the third of five brothers. Two of his brothers are dead and two others are serving time in prison. Mark states that his family has always been considered "white trash," although his father always worked in the oil fields. But because oil booms came and went in West Texas, the family had many "down" years.

Mark was eight years old when he broke into a house with the encouragement of a male neighbor in his thirties. The target site was three blocks from his own home. Mark asserts:

I had gotten into sniffing paint and glue and I was real high when this guy I was running with wanted me to go in this house and get a stereo for him. It was about midnight and since the people were there and I was so small, I pulled my shoes off and slipped through the back window, opened the back door and got the stereo. That's how I started doing it. I was pretty high.

Mark and his older mentor began burglarizing about one house per week. Mark's job was to enter the dwelling and pass the merchandise out the window to his partner. Another older male neighbor entered the partnership and they began sending Mark down air conditioning vents of drug stores, hardware stores, and restaurants. Where necessary, they'd lower him with ropes. They told Mark what to do and what to get. He averaged about fifty burglaries a year over the next ten years. When he was eighteen he was arrested the first time for burglary. He was placed on probation. Soon afterward he stole a truck while intoxicated on alcohol and drove to Dallas, where he was subsequently caught. They revoked his probation for the earlier arrest and he was sent to prison for three and a half years. Mark was released from prison in August 1976, and he spent only two days on the streets before he was arrested and later convicted for "cutting some dudes up over at the 'Spot' that was threatening my brother." He returned to prison for six and a half more years after those two days of freedom.

Out again in early 1983 he was free for 102 days until he was arrested for aggravated assault on a police officer. He spent an additional three and a half years in prison on a ten-year sentence. Ninety days after being released from his third incarceration, he was arrested for auto theft. He received a twenty-year sentence and served three and a half years. Thus since he was eight he has spent almost seventeen years in prison.

Mark reports always being high when breaking in to a target site. His biggest fear is of being shot by an unknown occupant, although he never carried a weapon himself:

Every time I've done a burglary I've been high. Because when I'm not high, I won't do it; because I'm too scared to do anything. I was always drunk or high on marijuana or acrylics; now heroin. It makes me not scared, you know. My biggest fear is being blown away. You know, somebody that's in there and has just been ripped off. They're thinking like me, you know, if I seen a suspicious character pull

up to my house and knock on the door, I wouldn't answer the door, I'd wait and if he came in my house I'd shoot him.

Although breaking into a house while high was certainly not unusual, Mark was unusual in that he performed all his burglaries at night, usually after 10:00 P.M. In addition, except for his youthful period working with the two older men, he never planned ahead, saying:

I never really planned a burglary. You know, unless it was a business like a drug store or a drive-in restaurant. We planned that. But as far as a house went, man, I'd just be cruising and see a house that looked empty and I'd stop and knock on the door. If nobody answered, you know, I'd go inside. Mostly I'm cruising. You see, as far as that goes, man, if I'm real sick, any house would be as good as the other one.

Mark is back in prison, having been sentenced for a third charge of theft of a motor vehicle. As his brother told us one day, "Mark will never make it in the free world, he never learned how."

BILLY

Billy is a novice burglar. He is a seventeen-year-old high school drop out. Billy was born and spent most of his life in Los Angeles. He recently moved to the local community to live with an aunt and uncle, having been expelled from school in California. He is on probation in California for "some minor stuff" and was allowed to move in an effort to get his life together away from the influences of friends in the Los Angeles area. He claims to have committed a number of burglaries in California with friends and a cousin there. He was entered into school locally but has since dropped out. He has not been arrested for any offenses since coming to Texas but has committed several burglaries. Unlike the other burglars in the study, he does not restrict himself to residential burglaries. He claims to have recently burglarized a music store, taking a number of musical instruments and selling them to friends. Billy does not appear to possess many skills as a burglar. He operates in a "smash and grab" manner, usually breaking a window and dashing in the dwelling, grabbing a few items, and running away. He does not have any reliable method of disposing of his stolen goods; instead he sells them on the street or gives them away to friends.

Appendix B

Detailed Research Methodology

The interviews and staged activity analyses followed the following format:

Staged activity analysis consists of extensive interviews and "ride-alongs," during which the informants were asked to discuss and evaluate residential sites they had previously burglarized and sites previously burglarized by other informants in the study. Each informant participated in as many as nine sessions with the researchers.

Session 1 consisted of a semistructured interview three to four hours in duration. During this session the informant was asked a series of open-ended questions ranging from queries about how he or she began as a burglar to specific questions about cues, motivations, probing strategies (casing), and disposing (fencing) of stolen goods. The remaining eight sessions involved actual visits to sites previously burglarized by the informant and other informants in the study. Sessions were conducted under all conditions in which burglars might conceivably commit their crimes: in the daytime, at night, with an informant alone, with informants grouped with their usual co-offenders, when using drugs, when stable, and when needing a drug administration (withdrawing). Before each session the informants were asked to estimate their own drug state at the time of the session and to recall their drug state at the time of the actual burglary of the site. An informant's drug state was estimated as follows:

1. Nonuser

2. Aroused: in need of a drug administration (sick or in the early stages of withdrawal)

3. Regular user/stable: having administered a drug recently and in no immediate need of another drug administration

4. Regular user/high: having administered a drug recently and feeling intoxicated, stoned, high, or nodding off

5. Intermittent user/stable: no drugs in the past twelve hours and no immediate need for drugs

6. Intermittent user/high: not a regular user but having administered a drug recently and feeling intoxicated, stoned, high, or nodding off

Session 2 was a daytime visit to at least one site previously burglarized ("hit") by the informant and to sites recently burglarized by others. The informants were then asked to direct the interviewer to the site of a recent burglary, using the method of travel and route taken at the time of the actual burglary. The informants were asked to recall why they had chosen that specific route and neighborhood or area of the city. Upon arriving in the general neighborhood of the target site the informants were instructed to proceed to the target site in as nearly as possible the same manner as they had at the time of the actual burglary. At the target site, the informants were asked a series of open-ended questions relating to the burglary, with emphasis on salient and subtle cues relied upon to select the target, including cues relating to occupancy, potential gain, and perceived risks. The informants were also queried about probes used to determine occupancy; method of entry, techniques of searching, division of labor (if co-offenders were involved), what was taken, the route and method of escape, how the stolen property was converted to cash or drugs, and how any money obtained by disposing of the stolen property was spent. Open-ended questions were pursued in detail depending upon the informants' willingness and ability to discuss each specific topic.

Following the interview, informants were asked to drive or walk through the immediate neighborhood and select a residence that they considered a high-risk site, that is, one that they were very unlikely to burglarize. After this selection the informants were asked why they rejected the high-risk site and what would need to be different in order to consider the site a good target for burglary.

Each informant was then driven to at least two sites previously burglarized by other informants and to at least two sites selected by their informants as high risk. At each previously burglarized site and matched high-risk site, the informant was asked to rate the site in terms of its vulnerability and attractiveness as an immediate burglary target given the circumstances that prevailed at the time of the staged activity analysis. The sites were rated on a scale of 0 to 10. An *attractiveness rating* of zero meant, "Under the circumstances that are present, I would not burglarize this residence." A rating of 10 meant, "This a very attractive and vulnerable target and I would definitely take steps to burglarize it *right now*." In addition, each informant was presented with two hypothetical situations and asked to provide an attractiveness rating for each: (1) If you knew no one was at home at this residence, what rating would you give the site on attractiveness as a burglary target *right now*; and (2) if you

knew no one was home and you knew that there was $250 in cash inside, what rating would you give the residence on its attractiveness as a burglary target *right now?* Thus Session 2 consisted of evaluating at least two previously burglarized sites and at least two sites selected by informants as high risk. All Session 2 sites were evaluated during daylight hours.

Session 3 was conducted in essentially the same manner, except that it was a group session. The informant was grouped with his or her co-offenders, if any. The purpose of this session was to determine to what extent, if any, group decisions differed from individual decisions. During group sessions the informants were asked to provide individual attractiveness ratings of the various sites without discussion with their co-offender(s). The informants were then encouraged to discuss the target site with their co-offender(s) and arrive at a group attractiveness rating. The drug state of each member was determined prior to evaluating the sites.

Session 4 took place at night. The informants evaluated sites they had previously burglarized at night (if any) and sites burglarized by others at night, along with their matched high-risk counterparts.

Session 5 was a group night session. Session 6 was an individual day session. Session 7 was a group day session. Session 8 was an individual night (and debriefing) session, and Session 9 was a group night (and debriefing) session. All sessions followed the same format as Sessions 1 through 4.

At the conclusion of Session 9 informants had evaluated up to twenty-one previously burglarized sites and their matched high-risk counterparts. Informants who never worked with partners and those whose partners refused to cooperate did not participate in Session 3, 5, and 9, and informants who burglarized only in the daytime did not participate in night sessions and vice versa. Three hundred and ten session hours with three active burglars were conducted. Each session was tape recorded and verbatim transcripts were made.

References

❖

Adams, Douglas (2000). Opportunity structure for deviance. In Patricia Adler, Peter Adler, and Jay Corzine (Eds.), *Encyclopedia of Crime and Deviance*. Philadelphia, Penn.: Brunner-Routledge.

Akers, Ronald L. (1985). *Deviant Behavior: A Social Learning Approach* (3rd Ed.). Belmont, CA: Wadsworth.

Akers, Ronald L. (1997). *Criminological Theories: Introduction & Evaluation.* Los Angeles: Roxbury.

Åkerström, M. (1983). *Crooks and Squares.* Land, Sweden: Studentlitteratur.

Allport, F. H. (1920). The influence of the group upon association and thought. *Journal of Experimental Psychology, 3.*

Atlas, Randal, and Will C. LeBlanc (1994). The impact on crime of street closures and barricades: A Florida study. *Security Journal, 5:* 140–5.

Barlow, H. D. (1990). *Introduction to Criminology* (4th ed.). Boston: Little, Brown.

Beavon, D. J. (1984). Crime and the Environmental Opportunity Structure: The Influence of Street Networks on the Patterning of Property Offenders. Unpublished master's thesis. Simon Fraser University, Burnaby, B.C.

Beck, A. J. (1989, April). Recidivism of prisoners released in 1983. Special report. Washington, D.C.: Bureau of Justice Statistics.

Becker, Gary (1968). Crime and punishment: An economic approach. *Journal of Political Economy, 76:* 169–217.

Bennett, T. (1986). A decision-making approach to opioid addiction. In D. Cornish and R. V. Clarke (Eds.), *The Reasoning Criminal.* New York: Springer.

Bennett, T. and R. Wright (1984). *Burglars on Burglary: Prevention and the Offender.* Aldershot, U.K.: Gower.

Bevis, C. and J. B. Nutter (1977). "Changing Street Layouts to Reduce Residential Burglary." Paper presented at American Society of Criminology annual meeting, Atlanta, GA.

Blakely, R., and M. Goldsmith (1976). Criminal redistribution of stolen property: The need for law reform. *Michigan Law Review*, 74: 1511–1613.

Blumstein, A. J., Cohen, and D. Farrington (1988). Criminal career research: Its value for criminology. *Criminology*, 26: 1–37.

Brantingham, P. L., and P. J. Brantingham (1975). Residential burglary and urban form. *Urban Studies*, 12: 273–86.

Brantingham, P. J., and P. L. Brantingham (1978). A theoretical model of crime site selection. In M. D. Krohn and R. L. Akers (Eds.), *Crime, Law and Sanctions*. Beverly Hills, Calif.: Sage.

Brantingham, P. J., and P. L. Brantingham (1981). *Environmental Criminology*. Beverly Hills, Calif.: Sage.

Brantingham, P. J., and P. L. Brantingham (1991). *Environmental Criminology*. Prospect Heights, IL.: Waveland Press.

Brantingham, Patricia L., and Paul J. Brantingham (1993). Nodes, paths and edges: Considerations on the complexity of crime on the physical environment. *Journal of Environmental Psychology*, 13: 3–28.

Brezina, Timothy (2002). Assessing the rationality of criminal and delinquent behavior: A focus on actual utility. In Alex R. Piquero and Stephen G. Tibbets (Eds.), *Rational Choice and Criminal Behavior: Recent Research and Future Challenges*. New York: Routledge. pp. 241–64.

Brown, B. B., and I. Altman (1981). Territoriality and residential crime: A conceptual framework. In P. J. Brantingham and P. L. Brantingham (Eds.), *Environmental Criminology*. Beverly Hills, Calif.: Sage.

Bureau of Justice Statistics (1988). *BJS Data Report, 1988*. Washington, D.C.: U.S. Department of Justice.

Bureau of Justice Statistics (1997). *Sourcebook of Criminal Justice Statistics, 1996*. Washington, D.C.: U.S. Department of Justice.

Cameron, M. O. (1964). *The Booster and the Snitch*. Glencoe, Ill.: Free Press.

Chaiken, J. M., and M. R. Chaiken (1982). *Varieties of Criminal Behavior*. Santa Monica, Calif.: Rand.

Chappell, R., and M. Walsh, (1974). Receiving stolen property: The need for systematic inquiry into the fencing process. *Criminology*, 11:

Cisneros, Henry G. (1995). *Defensible Space: Deterring Crime and Building Community*. Washington, D.C.: U.S. Department of Housing and Urban Development.

Clarke, Ronald V. (1997). *Situational Crime Prevention: Successful Case Studies*, (2nd Ed.). Guilderland, New York: Harrow and Heston.

Clarke, R. V., and D. B. Cornish (1985). Modeling offenders' decisions: A framework for policy and research. In M. Tonry and N. Morris (Eds.), *Crime and Justice: An Annual Review of Research* (4th ed.). Chicago: University of Chicago Press.

Clarke, R. V., and D. B. Cornish. Rational Choice. In R. Paternoster and R. Bachman (Eds.), *Explaining Crime and Criminals*. Los Angeles: Roxbury.

Cohen, L., and K. Land (1987). Age structure and crime. *American Sociological Review*, 52: 170–83.

Cohen, L. E., and M. Felson (1979). Social change and crime rates trends: A routine activity approach. *American Sociological Review*, 44: 588–608.

Cook, P. J. (1980). Research in criminal deterrence: Laying the groundwork for the second decade. In M. Tonry and N. Morris (Eds.) *Crime and Justice: An Annual Review of Research* (Vol. 2). Chicago: University of Chicago Press.

Cook, P. J. (1989). The economics of criminal sanctions. In M. L. Friedlander (Ed.), *Sanctions and Rewards in the Legal System: A*

Multidisciplinary Approach. Toronto: University of Toronto Press.

Cornish, Derek B. (1993). "Theories of action in criminology: learning theory and rational choice approaches." In *Advances in Criminological Theory, Vol. 5. Routine Activity and Rational Choice* ed. by Ronald V. Clarke and Marcus Felson, 351–382. New Brunswick, NJ: Transaction.

Cornish, D. B., and R. V. Clarke (1986). Situational prevention, displacement of crime and rational choice theory. In K. Heal and G. Laycock (Eds.), *Situational Crime Prevention: From Theory into Practice.* London: HMSO.

Cornish, D. B. and R. V. Clarke (Eds.). (1986). *The Reasoning Criminal: Rational Choice Perspectives on Offending.* New York: Springer Verlag.

Cromwell, Paul, and Karen McElrath (1994). Buying stolen property: An opportunity perspective. *Journal of Research in Crime and Delinquency, 31:* 295–310.

Crowe, T. O., and D. Zahm (1994). *Crime Prevention through Environmental Design.* Land Development 7: 22–27.

Easterbrook, J. A. (1959). The effect of emotion on cue utilization and the organization of behavior. *Psychological Review, 66:* 183–201.

Eich, E. (1989). Theoretical issues in state dependent memory. In H. I. Roediger, III and F. I. M. Craik (Eds.), *Varieties of Memory and Consciousness.* Hilldale, N.J.: Erlbaum

Farrington, D. (1986). Age and crime. In M. Tonry and D. Farrington (Eds.), *Crime and Justice: An Annual Review of Research.* Chicago: University of Chicago Press.

Faupel, C. E. (1987). Heroin use and street crime. *Qualitative Sociology, 10:* 115–31.

Faupel, C. E., and C. B. Klockars (1987). Drugs–crime connections: Elaborations from the life histories of hard-core heroin addicts. *Social Problems, 340:* 54–68.

Federal Bureau of Investigation (2001). *Crime in the United States, 1999.*

Washington D.C.: U.S. Government Printing Office.

Felson, Marcus (1998). *Crime and Everyday Life* (2nd ed.). Thousand Oaks, Calif.: Pine Forge.

Forrester, D., M. Chatterton, and K. Pease (1988). The Kirkholt Burglary Prevention Project, Rochdale. *Crime Prevention Unit Paper 13.* London: Home Office.

Freeh, Louis (1998). *Crime in the United States, 1997.* Washington D.C.: U.S. Department of Justice.

Gardiner R. A. (1978). *Design for Safe Neighborhoods.* Washington D.C.: Law Enforcement Assistance Administration.

Gaughan, J. P., and L. A. Ferman (1987). Issues and Prospects for the Study of Informal economics: Research Strategies and Policy. *Annals of the American Academy of Political and Social Science, 493:* 154–72.

Giallombardo, R. (1966). Interviewing in the prison community. *Journal of Criminal Law, Criminology and Police Science, 57:* 395–8.

Glassner, B., and C. Carpenter (1985). *The Feasibility of an Ethnographic Study of Property Offenders.* A report prepared for the National Institute of Justice (mimeo).

Glassner, B., M. Ksander, B. Berg, and B. Johnson (1983). A note of the deterrent effect of juvenile vs. adult jurisdiction. *Social Problems, 31:* 219–21.

Graham, J., and B. Bowling (1995). *Young People and Crime Survey 1992–93.* London: Home Office.

Greenberg, D. (1985). Age, crime and social explanation. *American Journal of Sociology, 91:* 1–21.

Hagedorn, J. (1990). Back in the field again: Gang research in the nineties. In R. Huff (Ed.), *Gangs in America.* Newbury Park, Calif.: Sage. pp. 210–59.

Hall, J. (1952). *Theft, Law and Society.* Indianapolis, Ind.: Bobbs-Metrill.

Hawkins, R., and G. P. Alpert (1989). *American Prison Systems: Punishment*

and Justice. Englewood Cliffs, N. J.: Prentice-Hall.

Henry, S. (1978). The Hidden Economy. London: Martin Robertson.

Hirschi, T. (1985). On the Compatibility of Rational Choice and Social Control Theories of Crime. Paper presented at the Home Office Conference on Criminal Decision Making, Cambridge, England.

Hirschi, T., and M. Gottfredson (1983). Age and the explanation for crime. American Journal of Sociology, 89: 552–84.

Inciardi, J. A. (1979). Heroin use and street crime. Crime and Delinquency, 25: 335–46.

Indermaur, David (1995). Violent Property Crime. Leichhardt, N.S.W.: The Federation Press.

Irwin, J. (1972). Participant observation of criminals. In J. Douglas (Ed.), Research on Deviance. New York: Random House.

Jackson, A. (1969). A Thief's Primer. New York: Macmillan.

Jacobs, Bruce A. (1999). Dealing Crack: The Social World of Streetcorner Selling. Boston: Northeastern University Press.

Jacobs, B., and R. Wright (1999). Stick-up, Street Culture and Offender Motivation. Criminology, 37(1) 149–73.

Jarbe, T. (1986). State-dependent learning and drug discriminative control of behavior: An overview. Acta Neurologica Scandinavica, 74. 37–59.

Jeffery, C. R. (1971). Crime Prevention through Environmental Design. Beverly Hills, Calif.: Sage.

Johnson, B. D., P. J. Goldstein, and N. S. Dudraine (1979). What is an addict? Theoretical perspectives and empirical patterns for opiate use. Cited by P. J. Goldstein in J. A. Inciardi (Ed.), The Drugs–crime Connection. Beverly Hills, Calif.: Sage.

Johnson, B. D., P. J. Goldstein, E. Preble, J. Schneider, D. S. Lipton, B. Spunt, and T. Miller (1985). Taking Care of Business: The Economics of Crime by Heroin Abusers. Lexington, Mass.: Lexington.

Kelling, G., and C. Coles (1996). Fixing Broken Windows. New York: Free Press.

Klockars, C. B. (1974). The Professional Fence. New York: Macmillan.

Lab, S. P. (1988). Crime Prevention: Approaches, Practices and Evaluations. Cincinnati, Ohio.: Anderson.

Lang, A. J., M. G. Craske, M. Brown, and A. Ghaneian (2001). Fear-related state dependent memory. Cognition and Emotion, 15(5): 695–703.

Lasley, James R. (1996). Using Traffic Barriers to "Design Out" Crime: A Program Evaluation of L.A.P.D.'s Operation Cul de Sac. Report to the National Institute of Design. Fullerton, Calif.: California State University Fullerton.

Lipton, Douglas, Robert Martinson, and Judith Wilks (1975). The Effectiveness of Correctional Treatment: A survey of Treatment Evaluation Studies. New York: Praeger.

Letkemann, P. (1973). Crime as Work. Englewood Cliffs, N.J.: Prentice-Hall.

Lowe, G. (1986). State-dependent learning effects with a combination of alcohol and nicotine. Psychopharmacology, 89: 105–7.

Maguire, Katherine, and Ann L. Pastore (Eds.). (1999). Sourcebook of Criminal Justice Statistics, (1998). Washington, D.C.: U.S. Department of Justice, Bureau of Justice Statistics.

Maguire, Mike (1982). Burglary in a Dwelling. London: Heinemann.

Martinson, Robert (1974). What works? Questions and answers about prison reform. Public Interest Vol. 25.

Matza, D. (1964). Delinquency and Drift. New York: Wiley.

McCall, G. J. (1978). Observing the Law. New York: Free Press.

McDonald, John M. (1980). Burglary and Theft. Springfield, Ill.: Charles C. Thomas.

Miethe, Terance D., and McCorkle Richard (1998). Crime Profiles: The Anatomy of Dangerous Persons, Places and Situations. Los Angeles: Roxbury.

Miller, W. B. (1958). Lower-class delinquency as a generating milieu of gang delinquency. *Journal of Social Issues*, 14: 5–19.

Myers, David G., and Helmut Lamm (1976). The group polarization phenomenon. *Psychological Bulletin*, 83: 602–29.

National Institute of Justice (1989a). *NIJ Reports, No. 213*. Washington, D.C.: National Institute of Justice.

National Institute of Justice (1989b). *NIJ Research in Action*. Washington, D.C.: National Institute of Justice.

National Institute of Justice (2000). *1999 Annual Report on Drug Use Among Adult and Juvenile Arrestees, Arrestees Drug Monitoring Program (ADAM)*. Washington, D.C.: U.S. Department of Justice.

Nee, C., and M. Taylor (1988). Residential burglary in the Republic of Ireland: A situational perspective. *The Howard Journal*, 27(2): 105–16.

Overton, D. A. (1964). State-dependent or "dissociated" learning produced with pentobarbital. *Journal of Comparative and Physiological Psychology*, 57: 3–12.

Preble, E., and J. J. Casey (1969). Taking care of business: The heroin user's life on the street. *International Journal of Addictions*, 4: 1–24.

Pruitt, D. G. (1971). Choice shifts in group discussion: An introductory review. *Journal of Personality and Social Psychology* 20: 339–60.

Rengert, George (1981). Burglary in Philadelphia: a critique of an opportunity structure model. In Paul J. and Patricia L. Brantingham (Eds.), *Environmental Criminology*. Beverly Hills, Calif.: Sage.

Rengert, G., and J. Wasilchick (1985). *Suburban Burglary: A Time and a Place for Everything*. Springfield, Ill: Charles C. Thomas.

Rengert, G., and J. Wasilchick (1989). *Space, time and crime: Ethnographic insights into residential burglary. A report prepared for the National Institute of Justice* (mimeo).

Reppetto, T. G. (1974) *Residential Crime*. Cambridge, Mass.: Ballinger.

Rubenstein, H., C. Murray, T. Motoyama, and W. V. Rouse (1980). *The Link Between Crime and the Built Environment: The Current State of the Knowledge (Vol. 1)*. Washington, D.C.: National Institute of Justice.

Sacco, V. R., and L. W. Kennedy (1994). *The Criminal Event*. Scarborough, Ontario: Nelson Canada.

Scarr, H. A. (1973). *Patterns of Burglary*. Washington, D.C.: U.S. Government Printing Office.

Shachmurove, Yochanan, Gordon Fishman, and Simon Hakin (1997). *The burglar as a rational economic agent*. CARESS Working Paper, 97–7. Mimeo.

Shaw, M. E. (1981). *Group Dynamics: The Psychology of Small Group Behavior* (3rd ed.). New York: McGraw-Hill.

Shover, N. (1971). *Burglary as an occupation*. Doctoral dissertation, at the University of Illinois. Ann Arbor, Mich.: University Microfilms.

Shover, Neal (1991). Burglary. In Michael Tonry (Ed.), *Crime and Justice: A Review of Research (Vol. 14) Chicago: University of Chicago Press*. pp. 73–114.

Shover, Neal (1996). *The Great Pretenders: Pursuits and Careers of Persistent Thieves*. Boulder, Colo.: Westview Press.

Shover, Neal, and David Honakers (1992). "The socially bounded decision making of persistent property offenders" *Howard Journal of Criminal Justice*, 31: 276–294.

Siegel, L. (1989). *Criminology* (3rd ed.). St. Paul, Minn.: West.

Siegel, L. (1995). *Criminology* (5th ed.). New York: West.

Simon, H. A. (Ed.). (1982). *Behavioral Economics and Business Organization (Vol. 2)*. Cambridge, Mass.: MIT University Press.

Simon, Herbert A. (1983). *Reasoning in Human Affairs*. Oxford: Blackwell.

Smith, J. D. (1987). Measuring the informal economy. *Annals of the American Academy of Political and Social Science*, 493: 83–99.

Smith, P. Z. (1993). *Felony Defendants in Large Urban Counties*. Washington, D.C.: Bureau of Justice Statistics.

Spiegler, M. D., and D. C. Guevremont (2003). *Contemporary Behavior Therapy* (4th ed.). Belmont, Calif.: Wadsworth.

Steffensmeier, D. (1986), *The Fence: In the Shadow of Two Worlds*. Totowa, N.J.: Rowman and Littlefield.

Steffensmeier, D., E. A. Allen, M. Harer, and C. Streifel (November 1987). *Age and the Distribution of Crime: Variant or Invariant.* Paper presented at the meeting of the American Society of Criminology. Montreal, Canada.

Stimson, G. V., and E. Oppenheimer (1975). *Heroin Addiction and Control in Britain.* London: Tavistock.

Sutherland, E. H. (1937). *The Professional Thief.* Chicago: University of Chicago Press.

Sutton, M. (1988). Handling Stolen Goods & Theft: A Market Reduction Approach. *Home Office Research Study, No 178.* London: Home Office.

Sutton, Mike, Jacqueline Schneider, and Sarah Hetherington (July 2001). Tackling Stolen Goods with the Market Reduction Approach. *Briefing Note. Paper 8.* London: Home Office.

Taylor, B., and T. Bennett (1999). Comparing Drug Use Rates of Detained Arrestees in the United States and England. Washington, D.C.: U.S. Department of Justice.

Taylor, M., and C. Nee (1998). The role of cues in simulated residential burglary. *British Journal of Criminology,* 238: 396–401.

Tittle, C. (1988). Two empirical regularities (maybe) in search of an explanation: Commentary on the age/crime debate. *Criminology,* 26: 75–85.

Tittle, C. R., and C. H. Logan (1973). Sanctions and deviance: Evidence and remaining questions. *Law and Society Review,* 7: 371–92.

Trasler, G. (1987). Cautions for a biological approach to crime. In S. Mednick, T. Moffitt, and S. Stack (Eds.), *The Causes of Crime: New Biological Approaches.* Cambridge, England: Cambridge University Press.

Tunnell, Kenneth D. (1992). *Choosing Crime: The Criminal Calculus of Property Offenders.* Chicago: Nelson-Hall.

Vold, G., and T. J. Bernard. (1986). *Theoretical Criminology* (3rd ed.). New York: Oxford University Press.

Walsh, D. P. (1980). *Break-ins: Burglary from Private Houses.* London: Constable.

Walsh, M. (1977). *The Fence: A New Look at the World of Property Theft.* Westport, Greenwood.

West, W. G. (1978). The short-term careers of serious thieves. *Canadian Journal of Criminology,* 20: 169–90.

Wilson, J. Q., and R. Hernstein (1985). *Crime and Human Nature.* New York: Simon and Schuster.

Wolfgang, M., R. Figlio, and T. Sellin (1972). *Delinquency in a Birth Cohort.* Chicago: University of Chicago Press.

Wright, R., and R. H. Logic (1988). How young house burglars choose targets. *The Howard Journal,* 27(2): 92–103.

Wright, Richard T., and Scott H. Decker (1994). *Burglars on the Job: Street Life and Residential Burglary.* Boston: Northeastern University Press.

Zajonc, R. B. (1965). Social facilitation. *Science,* 149: 269–74.

Zajonc, R. B. (1980). Feeling and thinking: Preferences need no inference. *American Psychologist,* 35: 151–75.

Zimring, F. E., and G. J. Hawkins (1973). *Deterrence: The Legal Threat of Crime Control.* Chicago: University of Chicago Press.

❖ Index